Home Library

EDITOR: Maryanne Blacker

FOOD EDITOR: Pamela Clark

∎ ∎ ∎

ART DIRECTOR: Robbylee Phelan

DESIGNER: Louise McGeachie

∎ ∎ ∎

ASSISTANT FOOD EDITORS: Jan Castorina, Karen Green

ASSOCIATE FOOD EDITOR: Enid Morrison

CHIEF HOME ECONOMIST: Kathy Wharton

HOME ECONOMISTS: Jon Allen, Jane Ash, Tikki Durrant, Sue Hipwell, Karen Hughes, Voula Mantzouridis, Alexandra McCowan, Louise Patniotis

EDITORIAL COORDINATOR: Elizabeth Hooper

KITCHEN ASSISTANT: Amy Wong

∎ ∎ ∎

STYLISTS: Rosemary de Santis, Carolyn Fienberg, Jacqui Hing, Anna Phillips

PHOTOGRAPHERS: Kevin Brown, Robert Clark, Andre Martin, Robert Taylor, Jon Waddy

∎ ∎ ∎

NUTRITION CONSULTANTS: Isobel Brown, Kathy Usic

∎ ∎ ∎

HOME LIBRARY STAFF:

SUB-EDITOR: Bridget van Tinteren

EDITORIAL COORDINATOR: Fiona Nicholas

∎ ∎ ∎

ACP PUBLISHER: Richard Walsh

ACP DEPUTY PUBLISHER: Nick Chan

∎ ∎ ∎

Produced by The Australian Women's Weekly Home Library.
Typeset by ACP Color Graphics Pty Ltd.
Printed by Times Printers Pte. Ltd, Singapore.
Published by ACP Publishing Pty Ltd, 54 Park Street, Sydney.

♦ **U.S.A.:** Distributed for Whitecap Books Ltd by
Graphic Arts Center Publishing, 3019 N.W. Yeon,
Portland, OR, 97210. Tel: 503-226-2402. Fax: 530-223-1410.

♦ **CANADA:** Distributed in Canada by Whitecap
Books Ltd, 1086 West 3rd.St,
North Vancouver BC V7P 3J6. Tel: 604- 980-9852.
Fax: 604-980-8197.

∎ ∎ ∎

Healthy Heart Cookbook
Includes index.
ISBN 1 86396 009 0.

∎ ∎ ∎

∎ ∎ ∎

COVER: Buttermilk Pancakes with Golden Pears, page 102.
OPPOSITE: Clockwise from back: Red Bell Pepper Soup,
Lentil Vegetable Soup, Potato Zucchini Vichyssoise, page 10.
BACK COVER: Beef and Pear with Garlic
Mustard Sauce, page 72.

Healthy Heart Cookbook

This wonderful book can help your heart to be healthier and give you a bonus of energy and well-being. You can plan meals using recipes from several sections, plus enjoy a terrific lunch for 10 or an easy dinner party. Our recipes are so tasty, tempting and nutritious that you'll never guess we've cut down on fat, a silent but serious trouble-maker for your heart and blood vessels. It's the fat you eat that can be transformed into cholesterol in your body, and it's vital to keep your cholesterol level down. Just by limiting your fat intake you begin to have control over your cholesterol.

Now turn the page for a guide to eating for a healthy heart.

Pamela Clark
FOOD EDITOR

Eating for a

It makes delicious sense to take care of your body and avoid the foods it doesn't like. One of the main offenders is fat, and here's why.

What you eat is a powerful key to health. Your body wants to be well, but often your eating habits create problems that could be avoided. This is because some substances in food are changed by the body's chemistry into other substances which have undesirable effects.

Fat is one of those substances. It can be transformed into excess cholesterol. Too much cholesterol in the blood can narrow and block arteries, leading to heart disease. The amount of cholesterol you produce depends on several factors, but mostly on the type of fat you eat. Cholesterol levels vary from one person to another. It is all very complex and not yet fully understood.

3 MAJOR HEALTH RISKS

A raised level of cholesterol in the blood, along with high blood pressure and tobacco smoking, make up 3 major risk factors for heart disease. As your blood cholesterol increases, your chances of dying from heart disease go up accordingly.

It is recommended that all adults should know their cholesterol level. A measurement of less than 200 milligrams per deciliter (mg/dl) of blood is desirable. Most cholesterol tests these days show both the High Density Lipoprotein (HDL) and Low Density Lipoprotein (LDL) readings. This is important as the levels of these components have a significant effect on your risk factor. An LDL reading below 130mg/dl is desirable (100mg/dl being ideal). While an ideal HDL reading above 60mg/dl actually reduces heart disease (a desirable reading is above 35mg/dl).

The terms cholesterol, saturated fats, monounsaturated fats and polyunsaturated fats are often confusing.

CHOLESTEROL

Cholesterol has different sources. We all produce cholesterol naturally in our bodies; it is a white, fatty, waxy substance essential to life and is used, among other things, to make cell walls and hormones.

It is also found in all foods of animal origin such as meat, poultry, milk, butter, cheese, cream and eggs. Dietary cholesterol, the amount of cholesterol actually present in foods, mostly has a minimal effect on blood cholesterol and is less important than total fat intake in determining blood cholesterol readings.

SATURATED FATS

These are found mainly in animal foods such as butter, cream, milk, cheese, egg yolks, variety meats, meat and processed meat products. They are also found in cakes, chocolates, cookies, potato chips, ice cream, French fries and pies. Vegetable sources of saturated fats are coconut oil and palm oil in certain products containing them. Check the labels of prepared foods.

Basically, when you eat these foods containing saturated fats, the body uses the fat to make cholesterol.

Some people make more cholesterol than others.

In the typical American diet, too much fat is eaten, particularly these saturated fats, which can result in raised blood cholesterol levels. Approximately half the population have a blood cholesterol above the desirable level of 200mg/dl.

MONOUNSATURATED FATS

These are found in foods including avocados, olives, peanuts, canola oil, olive oil and peanut oil. These fats lower the LDLs while at the same time leaving the HDLs unchanged. It is beneficial to include a small amount of these fats in the diet. Remember they are high in calories as are all fats.

POLYUNSATURATED FATS

These are found mostly in vegetable foods and polyunsaturated vegetable oils such as safflower, sunflower, maize or corn, soy bean and grape seed, and polyunsaturated margarine. These fats usually lower total cholesterol (both the LDLs and the HDLs). Polyunsaturated fats are also high in calories. Eat less of these than monounsaturated fat.

YOUR DAILY FAT INTAKE

A reasonable total fat intake is approximately 90 grams for the average man, and 68 grams daily for the average woman. The average American's diet consists of about 37% fat. If you follow our guidelines, you will be reducing that intake by around a quarter; to about 30% daily caloric intake of fat in your diet. It is even more desirable to lower fat intake to 20-25% daily caloric intake.

It is best to eat a limit of 5oz lean meat per serve. Meat should be trimmed of all visible fat, and allowance has been made for the varying percentage of fat which remains after trimming.

THE HEART SYMBOLS

The fat content of our recipes has been carefully calculated, and the fat grams per portion are given at the end of each recipe. The heart symbols given below are a quick guide to the fat content per portion of each recipe:

♥ ♥ ♥ = 5 grams and below
♥ ♥ = over 5 grams to 10 grams
♥ = more than 10 grams

As well, you can use the fat content chart to check some basic foods. A lot of fat is hidden in foods you buy, so it's worth checking labels.

HEALTHY HEART GUIDELINES

♥ Keep to a healthy weight – find out your healthy weight range and stay within that range.

♥ Eat a wide variety of fresh foods.

♥ Eat fewer fatty foods – check labels, avoid deep-fat frying.

♥ Eat more fruit, vegetables, bread and cereals – it is important to increase the amount of soluble fiber in the diet, such as oatmeal and oat bran.

♥ Cut down salt intake – use herbs and spices to add flavor to cooking.

♥ Drink less alcohol – only a small amount has been shown to be beneficial.

♥ Do not smoke – smokers have lower HDLs than nonsmokers.

♥ Exercise daily – aerobic exercise helps to increase HDLs.

Note: The figures at right show an average fat content of products. Variations will occur between brands.

healthy heart

APPROXIMATE FAT CONTENT PER 3½OZ OF FOOD

BEEF – uncooked, lean	Fat (g)
Boneless top blade steak	5.0
Boneless chuck	2.9
Boneless top sirloin steak	3.0
Tenderloin steak	4.4
Top round steak	3.2

COOKIES, CAKES and PASTRIES

Cookies, sweet, sandwich	24.0
sweet, plain	9.0
Cake, plain	17.0
fruit, rich	11.0
Crackers, cheese (10)	6.7
Cheesecake	35.0
Fruit pie	16.0

BREADS and CEREALS

Bread, pocket	1.4
white	2.0
whole-wheat	2.0
Bread crumbs	4.4
Corn Flakes	0.4
Puffed wheat	1.4
Flour, white	1.7
whole-wheat	2.5
Granola, natural	9.0
toasted	20.0
Pasta/noodles, uncooked	1.3
Rice, brown, uncooked	0.6
white, uncooked	0.2
Oatmeal, uncooked	7.8
Unprocessed bran, wheat	6.0
oat	8.6
Wheat germ	7.0

CONFECTIONERY

Hard candy	–
Chocolate, plain	31.0
Marshmallows (without coconut)	–

DAIRY FOODS

Butter	82.0
Buttermilk	2.0
Cheese, cheddar	33.0
creamed cottage	5.5
lowfat cottage	1.0
mozzarella, reduced fat	19.2
Parmesan	31.5
reduced fat cheddar	24.0
reduced fat feta	14.5
reduced fat ricotta	8.5
Cream, heavy (36% fat)	36.0
light sour	18.5
sour	35.0
Ice cream	6.5
Milk, full cream	4.0
reduced fat	1.5
skim	–
Yogurt, full cream, plain or flavored	4.0
skim, plain or flavored	–

EGGS	
Egg white	–
Egg, whole	11.0
Egg substitutes (check label)	0–10

FAST FOOD

Burrito (1)	13.6
Chicken, BBQ with skin	15.0
crumbed, fried	22.0
Fish, fried in batter	16.0
French fries	16.5
Fried rice	9.0
Hamburger, plain	10.0
Hot dog (1)	13.7
Hot fudge sundae (1)	10.9
Pizza	11.0

FRUIT

Avocado	22.0
Fruit, canned, dried, fresh and juice	–

LAMB – uncooked, lean

Sirloin chop	6.6
Fillet	3.6
Leg	2.2
Loin	3.9

LUNCHEON MEAT and SAUSAGE

Frankfurters	20.0
Salami	38.0
Sausages, beef, broiled	13.0
pork, broiled	24.0

NUTS – unroasted kernels

Almonds	54.0
Hazelnuts	36.0
Peanuts	49.0
Pecans	71.0
Pine nuts	51.0
Walnuts	52.0

OILS, FATS and DRESSINGS

Coleslaw dressing, reduced fat	4.5
Dripping, lard	100.0
Lowfat spread	40.0
Margarine, polyunsaturated	81.0
Mayonnaise, reduced fat	13.0
regular	49.0
Oil, olive	100.0
polyunsaturated	100.0
Salad dressings, Italian	37.0
no oil	–

PORK – lean

Bacon, untrimmed, broiled	35.0
Cooked ham	5.0
Pork butterfly chop, uncooked	1.0
Pork tenderloin, uncooked	1.7
Pork medallion, uncooked	2.2

POULTRY and GAME – uncooked, lean	
Chicken, breast	2.3
drumsticks, without skin	5.0
Quail	6.8
Rabbit	4.0
Turkey	2.2

SAUCES and SPREADS

Honey	–
Jam and preserves	–
Peanut butter	55.0
Soy sauce	–
Tomato paste	–
Tomato ketchup	–

SEAFOOD – uncooked

Cod, Atlantic	0.7
Flounder	1.4
Halibut	2.8
Mullet	1.8
Mussels	2.0
Ocean perch	1.8
Oysters	1.0
Salmon, canned	5.0
smoked	5.0
Sea scallops	1.0
Shrimp	1.0
Tuna, canned in oil	22.0
canned in water/brine	3.0
Whiting	0.5

VEAL – uncooked, lean

Chops	1.5
Steak	1.8

VEGETABLES

Garbanzo beans	5.7
Lentils	1.1
Potato, fries	15.0
roasted	5.0
Soy beans	5.0
Vegetables, canned	–
fresh	–
frozen	–

MISCELLANEOUS

Popcorn, plain	5.0
Potato chips	34.0
Sugar	–
Tofu	5.0

Breakfast

♥ ♥ ♥
CITRUS COMPOTE

Recipe can be made a day ahead.

2 grapefruit, segmented
2 tangerines, segmented
2 oranges, segmented
¼ cup fresh orange juice
2 teaspoons granulated sugar
½ cup fresh mint leaves

Combine fruit in bowl. Add juice to sugar in pan, stir over low heat until sugar is dissolved. Blend or process juice mixture and mint until mint is finely chopped; pour over fruit. Serve with thin blanched strips of orange and lemon peel, if desired.

Serves 2.

■ Not suitable to freeze.
■ Suitable to microwave.
  Total fat: Negligible.

♥ ♥ ♥
TOASTED GRANOLA

Granola can be refrigerated in an airtight container for several weeks.

1 cup old-fashioned oats
¼ cup unprocessed bran
¼ cup chopped dried apricots
¼ cup chopped dried apples
3 tablespoons golden raisins
4 teaspoons honey
4 teaspoons water
1 cup skim milk

Combine oats, bran and fruit in bowl, stir in combined honey and water. Spread mixture onto baking sheet, bake in 300°F oven about 45 minutes or until toasted, stirring occasionally. Serve granola with the milk or with fruit juice, if preferred.

Serves 2.

■ Not suitable to freeze.
■ Not suitable to microwave.
  Total fat: 9.7 grams.
■ Fat per serve: 4.8 grams.

♥ ♥ ♥
WHOLE-WHEAT RAISIN MUFFINS

Muffins can be made a day ahead.

½ cup whole-wheat flour
1½ teaspoons double-acting baking powder
¾ cup old-fashioned oats
4 teaspoons honey
¼ cup finely chopped dark seedless raisins
½ cup buttermilk
3 egg whites

Combine sifted flour and baking powder, oats, honey and raisins in bowl. Stir in combined buttermilk and egg whites; stir until just combined. Spoon mixture evenly into 8 x ⅓ cup nonstick muffin tins, bake in 375°F oven about 25 minutes or until well browned.

Makes 8.

■ Suitable to freeze.
■ Not suitable to microwave.
  Total fat: 10.5 grams.
■ Fat per muffin: 1.3 grams.

RIGHT: From left: Whole-Wheat Raisin Muffins, Citrus Compote, Toasted Granola.

WHOLE-WHEAT FRENCH TOAST

Make recipe just before serving.

4 slices whole-wheat bread
4 teaspoons skim milk
3 egg whites
3 tablespoons chopped fresh parsley
4 green onions, finely chopped

Cut rounds from bread using 3½ inch cutter; cut rounds in half. Dip halves into combined milk, egg whites, parsley and onions. Cook in heated nonstick griddle until lightly browned on both sides.

Serves 2.

- ■ Not suitable to freeze.
- ■ Not suitable to microwave.
- □ Total fat: 2.4 grams.
- ■ Fat per serve: 1.2 grams.

♥ ♥ ♥

BUCKWHEAT GRIDDLE CAKES WITH APPLE

Make recipe just before serving.

¼ cup buckwheat flour
¼ cup self-rising flour
4 teaspoons granulated sugar
½ cup skim milk
1 teaspoon light olive oil
1 egg white
3 tablespoons lowfat plain yogurt
⅛ teaspoon ground cinnamon

APPLE
1 apple
¼ cup water
2 teaspoons granulated sugar

Sift flours into bowl, stir in sugar, make well in center. Combine milk, oil and egg white; gradually stir into flour to make a smooth batter.

Drop tablespoons of batter into heated nonstick griddle, cook until bubbles appear, turn griddle cakes, brown on other side. Serve griddle cakes with apple and yogurt. Sprinkle lightly with cinnamon.

Apple: Peel, core and slice apple. Bring water and sugar to boil in pan, add apple pieces; simmer, covered, until apple is just tender.

Serves 2.

- ■ Not suitable to freeze.
- ■ Not suitable to microwave.
- □ Total fat: 5.1 grams.
- ■ Fat per serve: 2.5 grams.

♥ ♥ ♥

TOMATO MUSHROOM CUPS WITH BUTTERMILK DRESSING

Dressing can be made a day ahead. Make recipe just before serving.

6 large mushrooms
1 tomato, chopped

BUTTERMILK DRESSING
¼ cup buttermilk
1 green onion, chopped
½ teaspoon grated lemon zest
2 teaspoons fresh lemon juice
¼ teaspoon sugar
2 teaspoons nonfat dry milk

Remove stalks from mushrooms, fill with tomato. Place filled mushrooms on baking sheet, bake, uncovered, in 375°F oven about 10 minutes or until mushrooms are just tender. Serve mushrooms with buttermilk dressing.
Buttermilk Dressing: Combine all ingredients in bowl; refrigerate several hours or overnight.

Serves 2.

- ▨ Not suitable to freeze.
- ■ Suitable to microwave.
- ▢ Total fat: 1.1 grams.
- ■ Fat per serve: Negligible.

LEFT: Clockwise from back left: Whole-Wheat French Toast, Tomato Mushroom Cups with Buttermilk Dressing, Buckwheat Griddle Cakes with Apple.

♥ ♥ ♥
MANDARIN YOGURT CRUNCH

Make recipe close to serving.

1 cup lowfat plain yogurt
½ x 11oz can mandarin orange
**   segments, drained**
1 banana, sliced
2 teaspoons honey

TOPPING
3 tablespoons old-fashioned oats
¼ teaspoon ground cinnamon
1 teaspoon honey

Combine yogurt, mandarins, banana and honey in bowl, spoon into 2 serving dishes, sprinkle with topping.
Topping: Stir oats in pan over heat until lightly toasted; cool. Combine oats, cinnamon and honey in bowl.

Serves 2.

■ Not suitable to freeze.
■ Not suitable to microwave.
   Total fat: 2.1 grams.
■ Fat per serve: 1 gram.

♥ ♥ ♥
MINI SPINACH FRITTATA

Make recipe just before serving.

10 spinach leaves
½ teaspoon olive oil
1 small onion, sliced
4 teaspoons water
⅛ teaspoon ground nutmeg
2 egg whites
3 tablespoons skim milk
½ teaspoon olive oil, extra

Boil, steam or microwave spinach until tender, rinse under cold water; drain well, chop finely.

Heat oil in pan, add onion and water, cover, cook until onion is soft. Combine spinach, onion mixture, nutmeg, egg whites and milk in bowl.

Lightly grease 4 egg rings with a little of the extra oil. Add remaining extra oil to nonstick skillet, place egg rings in skillet, fill with egg mixture. Cook until mixture is set, remove egg rings, turn frittata, cook frittata until browned underneath.

Serves 2.

■ Not suitable to freeze.
■ Not suitable to microwave.
   Total fat: 4.5 grams.
■ Fat per serve: 2.2 grams.

♥ ♥ ♥
WHOLE-WHEAT ENGLISH MUFFINS

Muffins can be made 3 hours ahead.

1 package (¼oz) active dry yeast
3 tablespoons warm water
1 teaspoon sugar
1 cup all-purpose flour
1 cup whole-wheat flour
1 teaspoon sugar, extra
⅔ cup skim milk, warmed
4 teaspoons cornmeal
4 teaspoons polyunsaturated
**   margarine**

Combine yeast, water, sugar and 1 teaspoon of the all-purpose flour in bowl, cover, stand in warm place about 10 minutes or until mixture is frothy. Sift remaining flours into bowl, stir in yeast mixture, extra sugar and milk; mix to a firm dough. Knead dough on lightly floured surface about 7 minutes or until dough is smooth and elastic.

Return dough to bowl, cover, stand in warm place about 45 minutes or until dough doubles in size.

Knead dough on floured surface until smooth. Divide dough into 8 portions, roll out each portion to a 3 inch round. Dust both sides of rounds with cornmeal, place on tray. Cover, stand in warm place about 20 minutes or until rounds double in size.

Cook, covered, in nonstick skillet over low heat about 10 minutes each side or until lightly browned and cooked. Serve each muffin with ½ teaspoon margarine.

Makes 8.

■ Suitable to freeze.
■ Not suitable to microwave.
   Total fat: 24.4 grams.
■ Fat per muffin: 3 grams.

LEFT: Clockwise from back left:
Whole-Wheat English Muffins, Mandarin
Yogurt Crunch, Mini Spinach Frittata.

Snacks &

♥ ♥ ♥

LENTIL VEGETABLE SOUP

Soup can be made 2 days ahead.

1 teaspoon olive oil
1 clove garlic, minced
1 small onion, chopped
2 small carrots, chopped
2 small stalks celery, chopped
½ cup brown lentils
3 cups water
½ small chicken bouillon cube,
   crumbled
1 bay leaf
½ x 14½oz can no-added-salt
   tomatoes
2 teaspoons no-added-salt
   tomato paste
4 teaspoons chopped fresh parsley

Heat oil in pan, add garlic, onion, carrots
and celery, cook until onion is soft. Stir in
lentils, water, bouillon cube, bay leaf,
undrained crushed tomatoes and paste.
Bring to boil, simmer, covered, about 1½
hours or until lentils are soft. Discard bay
leaf. Stir in parsley just before serving.

Serves 2.

■ Suitable to freeze.
■ Suitable to microwave.
   Total fat: 5.6 grams.
■ Fat per serve: 2.8 grams.

♥ ♥ ♥

POTATO ZUCCHINI VICHYSSOISE

Recipe can be made a day ahead.

½ small leek, sliced
1 potato, chopped
¾ cup water
½ small chicken bouillon
   cube, crumbled
1 bay leaf
¼ teaspoon cracked black
   peppercorns
2 tablespoons buttermilk

ZUCCHINI SOUP
½ onion, chopped
4 zucchini, chopped
½ cup water
¼ small chicken bouillon cube,
   crumbled

Lunches

Combine leek, potato, water, bouillon cube, bay leaf and peppercorns in pan. Bring to boil; simmer, covered, about 20 minutes or until vegetables are soft. Discard bay leaf, cool slightly. Blend or process vegetable mixture with buttermilk until smooth; strain.

Pour this soup and zucchini soup into separate jugs, pour simultaneously into serving bowls. Pull skewer through both soups for a marbled effect.

Zucchini Soup: Combine onion, zucchini, water and bouillon cube in pan, bring to boil, simmer, covered, about 20 minutes or until zucchini is soft. Cool mixture slightly. Blend or process mixture until smooth.

Serves 2.

■ Not suitable to freeze.
■ Suitable to microwave.
  Total fat: Negligible.

♥ ♥ ♥
RED BELL PEPPER SOUP

Soup can be made 2 days ahead.

1 large red bell pepper, halved
1/2 teaspoon olive oil
1 small onion, chopped
2 cups water
1/2 cup vegetable juice
**1/2 small chicken bouillon
    cube, crumbled**
1/2 teaspoon sugar
1/4 cup lowfat plain yogurt

Broil pepper, skin-side-up, until skin blisters and blackens; peel away skin and chop pepper.

Heat oil in pan, add onion and pepper, cook, stirring, until onion is soft. Stir in water, juice and bouillon cube, bring to boil, simmer, covered, about 20 minutes or until pepper is soft.

Blend or process mixture until smooth, return to pan, stir in sugar. Stir until heated through, serve soup with yogurt.

Serves 2.

■ Not suitable to freeze.
■ Suitable to microwave.
  Total fat: 2.3 grams.
■ Fat per serve: 1.2 grams.

LEFT: Clockwise from back: Red Bell Pepper Soup, Lentil Vegetable Soup, Potato Zucchini Vichyssoise.

♥ ♥ ♥
FELAFEL WITH TOMATO CILANTRO SAUCE

Recipe can be made a day ahead.

1 cup (3½oz) dried garbanzo beans
½ onion, chopped
1 clove garlic, minced
3 tablespoons chopped fresh cilantro
½ teaspoon ground cumin
½ teaspoon garam masala
¼ teaspoon turmeric
2 teaspoons lowfat plain yogurt
1 egg white
1 cup shredded lettuce
2 whole-wheat pita pocket breads

TOMATO CILANTRO SAUCE
2 teaspoons cornstarch
1 cup water
4 teaspoons no-added-salt tomato paste
1 clove garlic, minced
4 teaspoons chopped fresh cilantro
3 tablespoons golden raisins

Cover beans with cold water in bowl, stand overnight; drain.

Cover beans with water in pan, bring to boil; simmer, uncovered, about 1 hour or until beans are soft. Drain beans, rinse under cold water; drain again.

Blend or process beans, onion, garlic, cilantro, spices, yogurt and egg white until smooth. Spread mixture evenly into shallow 8 inch x 12 inch baking pan, then turn onto lightly floured surface.

Cut into 20 rounds using 1½ inch cutter. Place rounds on baking paper-covered baking sheet, refrigerate 20 minutes. Bake felafel in 350°F oven about 20 minutes or until lightly browned. Serve felafel with lettuce in pocket breads topped with sauce.

Tomato Cilantro Sauce: Blend cornstarch with water, paste and garlic in pan. Stir over heat until mixture boils and thickens. Add cilantro and golden raisins.

Serves 2.

- ■ Not suitable to freeze.
- ■ Not suitable to microwave.
-   Total fat: 7 grams.
- ■ Fat per serve: 3.5 grams.

♥ ♥ ♥
CURRIED CHICKEN AND PASTA SALAD

Recipe can be made 3 hours ahead.

2 cups (5oz) pasta twists
½ x 15oz can crushed pineapple
¼lb boneless, skinless chicken breast half
2½oz mushrooms, sliced
2 green onions, chopped
4 teaspoons chopped fresh mint
2 lettuce leaves

DRESSING
1 teaspoon curry powder
¼ cup fresh lemon juice
1 teaspoon olive oil

Add pasta gradually to large pan of boiling water; boil, uncovered, until just tender. Drain, rinse under cold water, drain well.

Drain pineapple, reserve 4 teaspoons syrup. Poach, steam or microwave chicken until just cooked through; cool. Cut chicken into slices.

Combine pasta, pineapple, chicken, mushrooms, onions and mint in bowl. Add dressing, toss well; spoon into lettuce leaves just before serving.

Dressing: Combine all ingredients with reserved pineapple syrup in bowl.

Serves 2.

- ■ Not suitable to freeze.
- ■ Suitable to microwave.
-   Total fat: 9.4 grams.
- ■ Fat per serve: 4.7 grams.

ABOVE: Saucy Chicken Stir-Fry with Noodles.
LEFT: From Top: Curried Chicken and Pasta Salad, Felafel with Tomato Cilantro Sauce.

♥ ♥
SAUCY CHICKEN STIR-FRY WITH NOODLES

Make recipe just before serving.

5½oz boneless, skinless chicken breast half, poached
2 teaspoons olive oil
1 clove garlic, minced
1 teaspoon chopped fresh gingerroot
1 teaspoon sambal oelek
½ teaspoon curry powder
1 red bell pepper, chopped
½lb package fresh egg noodles
1 cup (2½oz) shredded cabbage
4 green onions, chopped
½ teaspoon cornstarch
¼ cup water
4 teaspoons reduced sodium soy sauce

Cut chicken into thin strips. Heat oil in wok or pan, add garlic, gingerroot, sambal oelek and curry powder; stir-fry until fragrant. Add pepper, noodles, cabbage, onions and chicken; stir-fry until heated through. Stir in blended cornstarch, water and sauce, stir until mixture boils and thickens.

Serves 2.

- ■ Not suitable to freeze.
- ■ Not suitable to microwave.
-   Total fat: 16 grams.
- ■ Fat per serve: 8 grams.

♥ ♥ ♥
CRUNCHY CARAWAY CRACKERS

Crackers can be made a week ahead.

¾ cup whole-wheat flour
2 tablespoons cornstarch
2 teaspoons nonfat dry milk
3 tablespoons cornmeal
¼ cup old-fashioned oats
½ teaspoon caraway seeds
4 teaspoons lowfat plain yogurt
¼ cup water, approximately

Sift flour and cornstarch, dry milk and cornmeal into bowl, stir in oats and seeds, make well in center. Stir in yogurt and enough water to mix to a firm dough. Knead dough gently on lightly floured surface until smooth. Roll out on lightly floured surface until 1/16 inch thick; prick all over with fork.

Cut rounds from dough using 1½ inch fluted cutter, place on ungreased baking sheets; bake in 350°F oven about 20 minutes or until lightly browned and crisp. Cool crackers on wire racks.

Makes about 36.

■ Suitable to freeze.
■ Not suitable to microwave.
□ Total fat: 4.9 grams.
■ Fat per cracker: Negligible.

♥ ♥ ♥
CHUNKY CHEESE DIP

Dip can be made several hours ahead.

8oz carton lowfat cottage cheese
½ small stalk celery, chopped
½ small carrot, chopped
½ small red bell pepper, chopped
1 green onion, chopped
1 small tomato, chopped
½ small green cucumber, chopped
4 teaspoons chopped fresh parsley

Combine all ingredients in bowl. Serve with fresh vegetables and the Crunchy Caraway Crackers, if desired.

Serves 2.

■ Not suitable to freeze.
□ Total fat: 2.5 grams.
■ Fat per serve: 1.2 grams.

RIGHT: From left: Chunky Cheese Dip, Crunchy Caraway Crackers.

♥ ♥
RICOTTA SPINACH GNOCCHI WITH CARROT SAUCE

Cook gnocchi just before serving.
Sauce can be made a day ahead.

1 small potato
10 spinach leaves, chopped
5oz reduced fat ricotta cheese
1 cup all-purpose flour

CARROT SAUCE
1 teaspoon olive oil
½ small onion, chopped
1 carrot, chopped
1 cup water
½ small vegetable bouillon
**   cube, crumbled**
1 teaspoon no-added-salt
**   tomato paste**
1 teaspoon cornstarch
2 teaspoons water, extra

Boil, steam or microwave potato until soft; drain, cool. Press potato through sieve into bowl, stir in spinach and cheese.

Knead in sifted flour ¼ cup at a time. Knead dough on lightly floured surface until smooth; shape dough into small balls. Place a ball of mixture into palm of hand, press with floured prongs of fork to make an indentation. Repeat with remaining balls of dough.

Add gnocchi to pan of boiling water, boil about 2 minutes or until gnocchi float to the surface; drain; keep warm. Serve gnocchi with sauce.

Carrot Sauce: Heat oil in pan, add onion, cook until soft. Add carrot, water, bouillon cube and paste. Bring to boil, cover, simmer until carrot is soft. Blend or process carrot mixture until smooth, return to clean pan. Stir in blended cornstarch and extra water, stir over heat until mixture boils and thickens slightly.

Serves 2.

■ Gnocchi suitable to freeze.
■ Not suitable to microwave.
　Total fat: 19.2 grams.
■ Fat per serve: 9.6 grams.

♥ ♥
VEGETABLE FRIED RICE

Recipe can be made 3 hours ahead.

3½oz no-cholesterol egg substitute,
**   lightly beaten**
1 onion, chopped
1 clove garlic, minced
1 teaspoon grated fresh gingerroot
3 tablespoons water
2 carrots, grated
½ small red bell pepper, chopped
3 zucchini, grated
1 stalk celery, thinly sliced
1 cup cooked rice
3 tablespoons reduced sodium
**   soy sauce**

Cook egg substitute in heated nonstick skillet until set, remove from skillet; chop. Combine onion, garlic, gingerroot and water in skillet, cook over heat until onion is soft. Add carrots, pepper, zucchini and celery, cook 2 minutes. Stir in rice, sauce and chopped omelet, stir over heat until heated through.

Serves 2.

■ Not suitable to freeze.
■ Suitable to microwave.
　Total fat: 11.2 grams.
■ Fat per serve: 5.6 grams.

♥ ♥
HERBED POTATOES

Make recipe just before serving.

3 large baking potatoes
¼ teaspoon paprika

FILLING
1 small carrot, chopped
2½oz broccoli, chopped
5oz reduced fat ricotta cheese
4 teaspoons chopped fresh chives

Scrub and dry potatoes. Prick potatoes all over with a skewer, bake in 350°F oven about 1 hour or until cooked.

Cut potatoes in half, scoop out flesh leaving ½ inch shell; reserve flesh.

Place shells on baking sheet, bake in 400°F oven 10 minutes. Spoon filling into shells, sprinkle with paprika. Bake in 350°F oven about 15 minutes or until hot.

Filling: Boil, steam or microwave carrot and broccoli until soft; drain. Beat cheese in small bowl until smooth, stir in potato flesh, carrot mixture and chives.

Serves 2.

■ Not suitable to freeze.
■ Not suitable to microwave.
　Total fat: 12.8 grams.
■ Fat per serve: 6.4 grams.

LEFT: Clockwise from front: Ricotta Spinach Gnocchi with Carrot Sauce, Herbed Potatoes, Vegetable Fried Rice.

♥ ♥ ♥
JELLIED GAZPACHO WITH PAPRIKA BREAD WEDGES

Recipe is best made a day ahead.

15oz can chicken consomme
¼ teaspoon tabasco sauce
4 teaspoons no-added-salt
  tomato ketchup
¼ cup tomato puree
½ carrot, chopped
½ cucumber, chopped
¼ red bell pepper, chopped
½ stalk celery, chopped
½ tomato, chopped
½ teaspoon sugar
4 teaspoons chopped fresh parsley
4 teaspoons unflavored gelatin
¼ cup water
1 lettuce leaf, shredded
2 teaspoons lowfat plain yogurt
2 black olives

PAPRIKA BREAD WEDGES
1 whole-wheat pita pocket bread
2 teaspoons water
1 teaspoon paprika

Combine consomme, tabasco, ketchup and puree in pan; bring to boil. Stir in carrot, cucumber, pepper, celery, tomato and sugar, bring to boil, simmer, uncovered, 5 minutes. Remove from heat, stir in parsley; cool.

Sprinkle gelatin over water in cup, stand in small pan of simmering water, stir until dissolved. Stir into vegetable mixture. Spoon mixture into 2 wetted molds (1 cup capacity), refrigerate until set. Turn molds onto plates, serve with paprika bread wedges, lettuce, yogurt and olives.

Paprika Bread Wedges: Cut pocket bread into 16 wedges. Brush each wedge with the water, sprinkle with paprika, place on baking sheet, bake in 350°F oven about 15 minutes or until browned and crisp.

Serves 2.

■ Not suitable to freeze.
■ Not suitable to microwave.
  Total fat: Negligible.

♥ ♥
BUTTERNUT TIMBALES WITH HERBED FLAT BREAD

Make recipe close to serving time.

½lb butternut squash, chopped
2 teaspoons olive oil
1 small onion, chopped
1½ tablespoons whole-wheat flour
2 egg whites, lightly beaten
½ vegetable bouillon cube, crumbled
1½ tablespoons grated Parmesan
  cheese

HERBED FLAT BREAD
¾ cup whole-wheat flour
2 teaspoons chopped fresh parsley
2 teaspoons chopped fresh basil
2 teaspoons chopped fresh rosemary
½ teaspoon olive oil
¼ cup lowfat plain yogurt
3 tablespoons water, approximately

Boil, steam or microwave squash until tender; drain.

Heat oil in pan, add onion, cook, stirring, until soft. Stir in flour, cook 1 minute, transfer mixture to bowl. Blend or process squash until smooth, stir into onion mixture with egg whites, bouillon cube and cheese; mix well.

Pour mixture into 2 lightly greased molds (½ cup capacity), cover with foil. Place molds in roasting pan, pour in enough boiling water to come half way up sides of molds. Bake in 325°F oven about 45 minutes or until set. Turn molds onto plates, serve with herbed flat bread.

Herbed Flat Bread: Combine sifted flour, herbs and oil in bowl, stir in yogurt with enough water to make a soft dough. Knead dough on lightly floured surface until smooth and elastic. Cut into 4 portions, knead each portion well. Roll each portion into a thin round, cook in heated nonstick skillet until golden brown patches appear underneath, turn and cook other side until golden brown.

Serves 2.

■ Not suitable to freeze.
■ Not suitable to microwave.
  Total Fat: 19 grams.
■ Fat per serve: 9.5 grams.

LEFT: Butternut Timbales with Herbed Flat Bread.
RIGHT: Jellied Gazpacho with Paprika Bread Wedges.

♥ ♥ ♥
CARROT ZUCCHINI GRIDDLE CAKES

Griddle cakes can be made several hours ahead.

2 green onions, chopped
1 small carrot, grated
1 small zucchini, grated
¼ cup self-rising flour
¼ cup whole-wheat self-rising flour
2 teaspoons granulated sugar
⅓ cup skim milk
1 egg white

Cook onions, carrot and zucchini in nonstick skillet about 5 minutes or until carrot is soft; cool.

Sift flours into bowl; stir in sugar, milk, egg white and carrot mixture. Drop tablespoons of mixture into heated nonstick griddle; cook until bubbles appear; turn griddle cakes, brown on other side.

Serves 8.

■ Not suitable to freeze.
■ Not suitable to microwave.
□ Total fat: 10.5 grams.
■ Fat per griddle cake: 1.3 grams.

♥ ♥ ♥
POTATO SALAD ROLLS

Recipe can be made 3 hours ahead.

12 large lettuce leaves
1 potato, chopped
2 green onions, chopped
4 teaspoons chopped fresh mint
4 teaspoons chopped fresh chives
1½oz reduced fat ricotta cheese
1 teaspoon honey
2 teaspoons lowfat plain yogurt

Cover lettuce leaves with boiling water in bowl; stand 1 minute. Drain, rinse leaves in iced water; drain on absorbent paper. Boil, steam or microwave potato until just cooked through.

Combine onions, mint, chives, cheese, honey and yogurt in bowl; stir in potato. Divide mixture between lettuce leaves, fold in sides, roll up tightly to enclose filling. Serve warm or cold.

Makes 12.

■ Not suitable to freeze.
□ Total fat: 3.4 grams.
■ Fat per serve: Negligible.

♥ ♥ ♥
CURRIED COLESLAW CUPS

Make recipe just before serving.

1 cup (2½oz) shredded cabbage
1 green onion, chopped
1 stalk celery, chopped
1 small carrot, grated
⅓ cup drained canned pineapple
   chunks
2 lettuce leaves

CURRY DRESSING
¼ cup lowfat plain yogurt
½ teaspoon curry powder
2 teaspoons white vinegar

Combine cabbage, onion, celery, carrot and pineapple in bowl. Add dressing; toss well. Spoon mixture into lettuce leaves.
Curry Dressing: Combine all ingredients in bowl; mix well.

Serves 2.

■ Not suitable to freeze.
  Total fat: Negligible.

LEFT: From top: Carrot Zucchini Griddle Cakes, Potato Salad Rolls, Curried Coleslaw Cups.

21

♥ ♥ ♥
VEGETARIAN ROLLS WITH SWEET AND SOUR SAUCE

Recipe can be prepared 3 hours ahead.

1 teaspoon olive oil
1 clove garlic, minced
2oz mushrooms, chopped
2 green onions, chopped
¼ red bell pepper, chopped
2 cups (5½oz) shredded
 Chinese cabbage
2 teaspoons water
2 teaspoons reduced sodium
 soy sauce
¼ small chicken bouillon
 cube, crumbled
4 teaspoons cornstarch
6 egg roll skins
1 egg white, lightly beaten

SWEET AND SOUR SAUCE
½ cup pineapple juice
3 tablespoons white vinegar
4 teaspoons no-added-salt
 tomato ketchup
2 teaspoons dark brown sugar
1 teaspoon cornstarch
1 teaspoon water

Heat oil and garlic in pan, add mushrooms, cook 2 minutes. Add onions, pepper and cabbage, cook, covered, until cabbage is wilted. Stir in blended water, sauce, bouillon cube and cornstarch. Divide mixture between skins, fold sides in, roll up firmly.

Brush rolls lightly with egg white, place on baking paper-covered baking sheet, bake in 375°F oven about 25 minutes or until lightly browned. Serve with sauce.
Sweet and Sour Sauce: Combine juice, vinegar, sauce and sugar in pan; blend cornstarch and water, add to pan, stir over heat until sauce boils and thickens slightly.

Makes 6.

▪ Not suitable to freeze.
▪ Not suitable to microwave.
 Total fat: 4.5 grams.
▪ Fat per roll: Negligible.

LEFT: Vegetarian Rolls with Sweet and Sour Sauce.

♥ ♥ ♥
CHILI PIZZA ROUNDS

Make recipe just before serving.

3 tablespoons chopped fresh chives
2oz lowfat cottage cheese
2 teaspoons chili sauce
4 teaspoons honey
4 teaspoons no-added-salt
    tomato paste
6 slices whole-wheat bread
4 teaspoons grated Parmesan cheese

Combine chives, cheese, sauce, honey and paste in bowl. Cut 2 inch rounds from bread, place rounds on baking sheets, toast in 350°F oven about 10 minutes.

    Spread rounds with prepared cheese mixture, sprinkle with Parmesan. Bake in 400°F oven about 10 minutes or until rounds are lightly browned.

Makes 6.

- Not suitable to freeze.
- Not suitable to microwave.
- Total fat: 7.4 grams.
- Fat per serve: 1.2 grams.

RIGHT: Chili Pizza Rounds.

♥ ♥ ♥
BAGEL CHIPS

Traditionally, bagels do not contain fat or animal products; these are the correct ones to use for this recipe. Store in airtight container for a month.

2 bagels
2 teaspoons olive oil
1 clove garlic, minced
¼ teaspoon dried oregano leaves

Using a serrated or electric knife, cut bagels into very thin slices. Place slices in single layer on baking sheets, very lightly brush 1 side of slices with combined oil, garlic and oregano. Bake in 325°F oven about 15 minutes or until lightly browned, cool chips on baking sheets.

Serves 2.

■ Not suitable to freeze.
■ Not suitable to microwave.
  Total fat: 9 grams.
■ Fat per serve: 4.5 grams.

♥ ♥ ♥
SALMON PARMESAN FINGERS

Make recipe just before serving.

2 slices whole-wheat bread
7½oz can salmon, drained
½ small stalk celery, finely chopped
2 teaspoons chopped fresh chives
4 drops tabasco sauce
4 teaspoons grated Parmesan cheese

Toast bread under heated broiler until lightly browned on 1 side. Combine salmon, celery, chives and tabasco in bowl. Spread salmon mixture on untoasted side of bread, sprinkle with cheese. Broil until lightly browned.

Serves 2.

■ Not suitable to freeze.
■ Not suitable to microwave.
  Total fat: 9 grams.
■ Fat per serve: 4.5 grams.

♥ ♥ ♥
FRUITY GINGERROOT BALLS

Recipe can be made 2 days ahead.

¼ cup chopped dried apricots
¼ cup chopped dried apples
¼ cup chopped pitted prunes
2 teaspoons chopped glace gingerroot
3 tablespoons nonfat dry milk
4 teaspoons corn syrup
2 teaspoons brandy
10 sliced almonds, toasted

Combine fruit, gingerroot, dry milk, syrup and brandy in bowl. Roll rounded teaspoons of mixture into balls with slightly wet hands. Top each fruity gingerroot ball with an almond slice.

Makes 10.

■ Not suitable to freeze.
  Total fat: Negligible.

♥ ♥
MINI ASPARAGUS QUICHES
Make quiches just before serving.

PASTRY
⅓ **cup whole-wheat self-rising flour**
⅓ **cup all-purpose flour**
1 teaspoon grated lemon zest
2 teaspoons fresh lemon juice
4 teaspoons corn syrup
1 egg white, lightly beaten
4 teaspoons water, approximately

FILLING
¼**lb fresh asparagus, chopped**
3½oz no-cholesterol egg substitute,
   lightly beaten
3 tablespoons grated reduced fat
   cheddar cheese
3 tablespoons buttermilk
4 teaspoons nonfat dry milk
4 teaspoons chopped fresh tarragon

Pastry: Sift flours into bowl, stir in combined zest, juice, syrup and egg white with enough water to make ingredients cling together (or process all ingredients until mixture forms a ball). Knead gently on lightly floured surface until smooth. Cover, refrigerate 30 minutes. Roll pastry until large enough to line 2 deep 3½ inch flan pans; trim edges.

Place asparagus into pastry cases, add filling. Place pans on baking sheet, bake in 400°F oven 10 minutes; reduce heat to 350°F, bake 25 minutes. Stand quiches 5 minutes, then carefully remove from pans. Return quiches to baking sheet, bake further 10 minutes or until pastry is cooked.
Filling: Boil, steam or microwave asparagus until soft; rinse under cold water, drain. Combine egg substitute and cheese in bowl, gradually stir in buttermilk, dry milk and tarragon.

Makes 2.

■ Not suitable to freeze.
■ Not suitable to microwave.
 Total fat: 18.8 grams.
■ Fat per quiche: 9.4 grams.

LEFT: Clockwise from front: Salmon Parmesan Fingers, Fruity Gingerroot Balls, Bagel Chips.
BELOW: Mini Asparagus Quiches.

Sandwich Fillings

♥ ♥ ♥
APRICOT RELISH OPEN SANDWICHES

Relish can be made 2 weeks ahead.

4 lettuce leaves
2 x 1½oz slices lean roasted beef
2 slices dark rye bread

RELISH
⅔ cup chopped dried apricots
⅓ cup dark brown sugar
2 teaspoons yellow mustard seeds
1 onion, sliced
⅔ cup water
⅓ cup cider vinegar

Place lettuce and beef on bread. Top each bread slice with 4 teaspoons of the relish. Keep remaining relish for future use.
Relish: Combine all ingredients in pan, stir over heat, without boiling, until sugar is dissolved. Bring to boil, simmer about 30 minutes or until thick, remove from heat, spoon into sterilized jar; seal while hot. You will have about 1 cup of relish.

Makes 2.

■ Not suitable to freeze.
■ Not suitable to microwave.
   Total fat: 5.8 grams.
■ Fat per sandwich: 2.9 grams.

♥ ♥
HERBED EGG SANDWICHES

Make sandwiches just before serving.

3½oz no-cholesterol egg substitute
2 teaspoons chopped fresh basil
4 teaspoons chopped fresh chives
4 teaspoons light sour cream
1 teaspoon seeded mustard
¼ cup alfalfa sprouts
4 slices rye bread

Combine egg substitute, herbs, cream and mustard in small pan, stir over low heat until mixture begins to set. Remove pan from heat, continue stirring until set. Spoon filling and sprouts onto 2 bread slices, top with remaining bread.

Makes 2.

■ Not suitable to freeze.
■ Suitable to microwave.
   Total fat: 16.5 grams.
■ Fat per sandwich: 8.3 grams.

♥ ♥
SPRING SALAD SANDWICHES

Filling can be made 3 hours ahead.

3½oz lowfat cottage cheese
8 spinach leaves, chopped
1 green onion, chopped
½ small carrot, grated
¼ cup mung bean sprouts
2 teaspoons sesame seeds, toasted
1 teaspoon fresh lemon juice
4 slices whole-wheat bread
¼ (1½oz) avocado

Combine cheese, spinach, onion, carrot, sprouts, seeds and juice in bowl. Spread bread slices with avocado, top with filling; then top with remaining bread.

Makes 2.

■ Not suitable to freeze.
   Total fat: 12 grams.
■ Fat per sandwich: 6 grams.

♥ ♥ ♥
CURRIED TUNA SANDWICHES

Filling can be made a day ahead.

1 small tomato, sliced
4 slices rye bread

FILLING
½ x 6oz can tuna in brine, drained, flaked
½ small stalk celery, chopped
½ teaspoon curry powder
4 teaspoons chopped fresh parsley
4 teaspoons reduced fat coleslaw dressing

Divide tomato and filling between 2 bread slices; top with remaining bread.
Filling: Combine tuna, celery, curry powder and parsley in bowl, stir in dressing; mix well.

Makes 2.

■ Not suitable to freeze.
   Total fat: 7 grams.
■ Fat per sandwich: 3.5 grams.

♥ ♥ ♥
CHICKEN CELERY SANDWICHES

Make sandwiches just before serving.

4 slices whole-wheat bread

SPREAD
7oz boneless, skinless chicken breast half
4 teaspoons fresh lemon juice
¼ cup lowfat plain yogurt
¼ teaspoon hot English mustard
1 stalk celery

Divide spread between 2 bread slices; top with remaining bread.
Spread: Poach, steam or microwave chicken until tender, cool; chop roughly. Blend or process chicken, juice, yogurt and mustard until combined, stir in celery.

Makes 2.

■ Not suitable to freeze.
■ Suitable to microwave.
   Total fat: 8 grams.
■ Fat per sandwich: 4 grams.

LEFT: Clockwise from front right: Chicken Celery Sandwiches, Herbed Egg Sandwiches, Apricot Relish Open Sandwiches, Curried Tuna Sandwiches, Spring Salad Sandwiches.

SALMON AND CUCUMBER SANDWICHES

Filling can be made 3 hours ahead.

3½oz can pink salmon, drained
4 teaspoons lowfat cottage cheese
1 small green cucumber, chopped
2 teaspoons chopped fresh chives
4 slices whole-wheat bread

Combine salmon, cheese, cucumber and chives in bowl; mix well. Spread mixture evenly over 2 bread slices, top with remaining bread.

Makes 2.

- Not suitable to freeze.
- Total fat: 9 grams.
- Fat per sandwich: 3.5 grams.

EGGPLANT TAHINI SANDWICHES

Filling can be made 3 days ahead.

4 slices whole-wheat bread
1 cup shredded lettuce
4 teaspoons chopped fresh mint

FILLING
1 eggplant
4 teaspoons tahini (sesame paste)
1 clove garlic, minced
2 tablespoons fresh lemon juice

Spread 2 bread slices each with 3 tablespoons of the filling. Top with lettuce and mint, then remaining bread. Keep remaining filling for future use.

Filling: Halve eggplant, place on baking sheet, bake in 375°F oven about 25 minutes or until soft, cool; remove skin. Blend or process eggplant, tahini, garlic and juice until well combined. You will have about 1 cup filling.

Makes 2.

- Not suitable to freeze.
- Not suitable to microwave.
  Total fat: 13.4 grams.
- Fat per sandwich: 3.3 grams.

FRUITY RICOTTA SANDWICHES

Spread can be made a week ahead.

3 tablespoons reduced fat
**   ricotta cheese**
4 slices whole-wheat bread

SPREAD
⅓ cup chopped dried apricots
3 tablespoons chopped dried apples
1 cup fresh orange juice
1¼ cups water

Divide cheese between 2 bread slices, top each slice with 4 teaspoons of spread; then remaining bread.

Spread: Combine all ingredients in pan, stir over heat until mixture boils, simmer, uncovered, about 20 minutes or until mixture thickens, stir occasionally; cool. Blend or process mixture until smooth, spoon into sterilized jar, seal while hot. You will have about 1 cup spread.

- Not suitable to freeze.
- Suitable to microwave.
  Total fat: 5.8 grams.
- Fat per sandwich: 2.9 grams.

COUSCOUS TABBOULEH POCKETS

Tabbouleh can be made a day ahead.

2 tablespoons couscous
¼ cup boiling water
½ cup chopped fresh parsley
1 small tomato, chopped
¼ small onion, chopped
4 teaspoons fresh lemon juice
1 teaspoon chopped fresh mint
2 whole-wheat pita pocket
**   breads, halved**
¼ (1½oz) avocado

Combine couscous and boiling water in bowl, stand 20 minutes or until water is absorbed; cool. Combine couscous, parsley, tomato, onion, juice and mint in bowl. Spread inside of breads with avocado, fill with tabbouleh.

Serves 2.

- Not suitable to freeze.
  Total fat: 12.4 grams.
- Fat per serve: 6.2 grams.

ABOVE LEFT: From top: Couscous Tabbouleh Pockets, Salmon and Cucumber Sandwiches, Fruity Ricotta Sandwiches. ABOVE RIGHT: Clockwise from back left: Pizza Pockets Filling, Eggplant Tahini Filling, Waldorf and Alfalfa Filling, Squash Coleslaw Filling.

♥ ♥ ♥
PIZZA POCKETS

Make filling close to serving time.

1 tomato, chopped
1 onion, chopped
3½oz button mushrooms, sliced
½ cup canned crushed pineapple
½ red bell pepper, chopped
1 clove garlic, minced
1 teaspoon dried oregano leaves
3 tablespoons grated Parmesan
    cheese
2 whole-wheat pita pocket
    breads, halved

Combine tomato, onion, mushrooms, drained pineapple and pepper in nonstick skillet, cook until vegetables are soft. Stir in garlic, oregano and cheese; cool. Spoon mixture into pocket breads.

Serves 2.

■ Not suitable to freeze.
■ Suitable to microwave.
   Total fat: 9 grams.
■ Fat per serve: 4.5 grams.

♥ ♥ ♥
SQUASH COLESLAW
SANDWICHES

Make sandwiches just before serving.

4 slices whole-wheat bread

COLESLAW
¾lb golden nugget squash, grated
½ small red bell pepper, chopped
1 cup (2½oz) sliced cabbage
2 zucchini, grated
¼ cup reduced fat mayonnaise
¼ teaspoon dry mustard

Divide coleslaw between 2 bread slices; top with remaining bread.
Coleslaw: Combine squash, pepper, cabbage and zucchini in bowl. Combine mayonnaise and mustard in bowl, stir into coleslaw; mix well.

Makes 2.

■ Not suitable to freeze.
   Total fat: 9.8 grams.
■ Fat per sandwich: 4.9 grams.

♥ ♥
WALDORF AND ALFALFA
SANDWICHES

Make filling just before serving.

4 slices whole-wheat bread
½ cup alfalfa sprouts

WALDORF FILLING
1 stalk celery, finely chopped
½ red apple, grated
3 tablespoons light sour cream

Spread waldorf filling evenly over 2 bread slices, top with alfalfa sprouts, then remaining bread.
Waldorf Filling: Combine all ingredients in bowl; mix well.

Makes 2.

■ Not suitable to freeze.
   Total fat: 11.4 grams.
■ Fat per sandwich: 5.7 grams.

Seafood

♥ ♥

FISH WITH PAPRIKA AND PIMIENTO SAUCE

Fish is best cooked close to serving time. Sauce can be made a day ahead.

2 x 7oz white fish fillets
½ x 13oz can pimientos, drained

SAUCE
2 teaspoons olive oil
1 small onion, chopped
2 teaspoons paprika
¾ cup water
½ vegetable bouillon cube, crumbled
2 teaspoons fresh lemon juice
1 teaspoon sugar

Poach or steam fish until just cooked. Cut half a pimiento into strips; reserve remaining pimientos for sauce. Place pimiento strips on fish; serve with sauce.
Sauce: Chop reserved pimientos. Heat oil in pan, add onion, cook until soft. Stir in paprika, cook, 30 seconds. Stir in pimientos and remaining ingredients, bring to boil, simmer, uncovered, 3 minutes. Blend or process mixture until smooth.

Serves 2.

- ■ Not suitable to freeze.
- ■ Suitable to microwave.
- ☐ Total fat: 11.8 grams.
- ■ Fat per serve: 5.9 grams.

♥ ♥ ♥

FISH IN WINE GARLIC MARINADE

Recipe can be prepared a day ahead.

2 x ½lb whole white flesh fish
1 clove garlic, minced
½ teaspoon grated lemon zest
3 tablespoons fresh lemon juice
4 teaspoons dry white wine
1 teaspoon olive oil
2 teaspoons chopped fresh thyme
½ teaspoon grated fresh gingerroot
½ teaspoon sugar

Place fish in shallow dish, pour over combined remaining ingredients, turn fish to coat in marinade; refrigerate several hours or overnight.
Remove fish from marinade, wrap in foil, place in roasting pan. Bake in 350°F oven about 20 minutes or until fish are just cooked through.

Serves 2.

- ■ Not suitable to freeze.
- ■ Suitable to microwave.
- ☐ Total fat: 6.6 grams.
- ■ Fat per serve: 3.3 grams.

♥ ♥

FISH CUTLETS WITH HERB CRUMBLE

Make recipe just before serving.

2 x ½lb white fish cutlets
¾ cup fresh whole-wheat
**   bread crumbs**
3 tablespoons fresh lemon juice
3 tablespoons chopped fresh parsley
4 teaspoons chopped fresh chives
1 clove garlic, minced

Cook fish under heated broiler 5 minutes, turn, sprinkle with combined bread crumbs, juice, herbs and garlic, cook about 5 minutes or until just cooked through and lightly browned.

Serves 2.

- ■ Not suitable to freeze.
- ■ Suitable to microwave.
- ☐ Total fat: 10.4 grams.
- ■ Fat per serve: 5.2 grams.

LEFT: Clockwise from back: Fish in Wine Garlic Marinade, Fish Cutlets with Herb Crumble, Fish with Paprika and Pimiento Sauce.

♥ ♥
TROPICAL FISH PATTIES

Recipe can be prepared a day ahead.

1lb white fish fillets
¾ cup canned crushed
   pineapple, drained
½ small red bell pepper, chopped
½ small green bell pepper, chopped
4 teaspoons chopped fresh chives
3 egg whites
1 cup (2½oz) fresh bread crumbs
¼ cup lowfat plain yogurt

Blend or process fish until smooth, combine with pineapple, peppers, chives, egg whites, bread crumbs and yogurt. Shape mixture into 8 patties, cook in heated nonstick skillet until well browned on both sides and cooked through.

Makes 8.

- ■ Not suitable to freeze.
- ■ Not suitable to microwave.
- ☐ Total fat: 11.6 grams.
- ■ Fat per serve: 5.8 grams.

♥ ♥
FISH CUTLETS WITH CILANTRO CHILI SAUCE

Make recipe close to serving time.

2 x 7oz white fish cutlets
1 small onion, sliced
½ cup water
¼ cup dry vermouth
1 tablespoon fresh lime juice
1 tablespoon olive oil
1 small fresh red chili, finely chopped
2 teaspoons all-purpose flour
½ vegetable bouillon cube, crumbled
4 teaspoons chopped fresh cilantro

Place fish in shallow ovenproof dish, top with onion. Pour over combined water, vermouth and juice, cover, bake in 350°F oven about 20 minutes or until fish is just cooked. Remove fish; keep warm. Strain and reserve liquid.

Heat oil in pan, add chili, cook 30 seconds, stir in flour, cook until bubbling. Remove from heat, gradually stir in reserved liquid and bouillon cube, stir over heat until mixture boils and thickens; stir in cilantro. Serve sauce over fish.

Serves 2.

- ■ Not suitable to freeze.
- ■ Suitable to microwave.
- ☐ Total fat: 18.7 grams.
- ■ Fat per serve: 9.4 grams.

♥ ♥
FISH TWISTS WITH BASIL AND PINE NUT DRESSING

Make recipe close to serving time.

2 x 5oz whiting fillets
1 tomato
1 eggplant

DRESSING
⅓ cup red wine vinegar
3 tablespoons honey
3 tablespoons chopped fresh basil
1 clove garlic, minced
4 teaspoons pine nuts, toasted

Cut each fillet lengthways into 3 strips. Cut tomato and eggplant into 6 slices each. Top eggplant slices with tomato and fish strips. Steam over simmering water about 5 minutes or until fish is just cooked. Serve with dressing.
Dressing: Combine all ingredients in bowl; mix well.

Serves 2.

- ■ Not suitable to freeze.
- ■ Suitable to microwave.
- ☐ Total fat: 11.5 grams.
- ■ Fat per serve: 5.6 grams.

♥ ♥
CHILI SEAFOOD RICE

Recipe can be made a day ahead.

2 teaspoons olive oil
1 small onion, chopped
1 clove garlic, minced
14½oz can no-added-salt tomatoes
1 small fresh red chili, finely chopped
¼ cup dry red wine
14oz can chicken consomme
½ cup long-grain rice
4 teaspoons chopped fresh parsley
1 small red bell pepper, chopped
1 small green bell pepper, chopped
¾lb white fish fillets, chopped
3½oz crab meat
¼lb sea scallops

Heat oil in pan, add onion and garlic, cook until soft. Add tomatoes, chili, wine and consomme, bring to boil, gradually stir in rice, simmer, uncovered, about 15 minutes or until rice is just tender. Add parsley, peppers and seafood, gently stir over heat about 5 minutes or until peppers are soft and seafood is just cooked.

Serves 2.

- ■ Not suitable to freeze.
- ■ Not suitable to microwave.
- ☐ Total fat: 13.5 grams.
- ■ Fat per serve: 6.8 grams.

ABOVE: Fish Twists with Basil and Pine Nut Dressing.
RIGHT: Clockwise from top: Chili Seafood Rice, Tropical Fish Patties, Fish Cutlets with Cilantro Chili Sauce.

♥ ♥

SPINACH AND BUTTERNUT RING WITH SCALLOP SAUCE

Make recipe close to serving time.

½ bunch (10oz) spinach

FILLING
1 teaspoon olive oil
5 green onions, sliced
13oz butternut squash, chopped
½ cup water
⅔ cup buttermilk
¼ cup nonfat dry milk
¼ teaspoon ground nutmeg
2 egg whites

SCALLOP SAUCE
1 teaspoon olive oil
5 green onions, sliced
4 teaspoons water
4 teaspoons all-purpose flour
1 cup skim milk
1 teaspoon no-added-salt tomato paste
3½oz sea scallops

Trim spinach leaves, place spinach in pan of boiling water until just wilted, drain, rinse under cold water; drain on absorbent paper. Lightly grease 8 inch savarin ring pan. Line pan with spinach leaves, allowing spinach to overhang edge of pan, spoon in filling, fold spinach over to enclose filling.

Cover pan with lightly greased foil, place in roasting pan with enough hot water to come half way up side of pan. Bake in 375°F oven about 45 minutes or until mixture is puffed slightly and set. Stand 5 minutes before turning out. Serve ring with warm scallop sauce.

Filling: Heat oil in pan, add onions and squash, cook until onions are soft. Add water, bring to boil, simmer, covered, about 15 minutes or until squash is soft; cool slightly. Blend or process squash mixture with buttermilk, dry milk and nutmeg until smooth; transfer mixture to bowl. Beat egg whites until soft peaks form, gently fold into squash mixture.

Scallop Sauce: Heat oil in pan, add onions and water, cook until soft, stir in flour, cook 1 minute. Remove from heat, gradually stir in milk and paste, stir over heat until mixture boils and thickens. Separate roe from scallops; push roe through fine sieve; thinly slice white part of scallops. Combine roe and white part of scallops with sauce mixture.

Serves 2.

- Not suitable to freeze.
- Not suitable to microwave.
- Total fat: 13.8 grams.
- Fat per serve: 6.9 grams.

♥ ♥

HEARTY OYSTER SOUP

Make recipe close to serving time.

2 teaspoons olive oil
1 small onion, chopped
1 clove garlic, minced
1¼ cups water
1 cup skim milk
½ vegetable bouillon cube, crumbled
2 potatoes, chopped
3 tablespoons no-added-salt tomato paste
¼ teaspoon cracked black peppercorns
12 oysters, shucked
4 teaspoons chopped fresh chives
4 teaspoons light sour cream

Heat oil in pan, add onion and garlic, cook until soft. Add water, milk, bouillon cube, potatoes, paste and peppercorns, bring to boil, simmer, covered, about 8 minutes or until potato is soft; cool slightly.

Blend or process undrained mixture until smooth, return to pan, add oysters and chives, stir over heat until soup is heated through. Serve soup topped with cream.

Serves 2.

- Not suitable to freeze.
- Not suitable to microwave.
- Total fat: 15.8 grams.
- Fat per serve: 7.9 grams.

♥

SALMON AND HERB SOUFFLES

Cook recipe just before serving.

7¾oz can salmon, drained
4 teaspoons chopped fresh chives
4 teaspoons chopped fresh parsley
⅛ teaspoon cayenne pepper
4 teaspoons polyunsaturated margarine
4 teaspoons all-purpose flour
½ cup skim milk
2 egg whites

Grease 2 souffle dishes (1 cup capacity). Combine salmon, herbs and pepper in bowl; mix well. Heat margarine in pan, stir in flour; cook until bubbling. Remove from heat, gradually stir in milk, stir over heat until sauce boils and thickens.

Stir sauce into salmon mixture. Beat egg whites in small bowl until soft peaks form, fold into salmon mixture. Spoon mixture into prepared dishes, bake in 350°F oven about 20 minutes or until risen and well browned.

Serves 2.

- Not suitable to freeze.
- Not suitable to microwave.
- Total fat: 27 grams.
- Fat per serve: 13.5 grams.

ABOVE: Spinach and Butternut Ring with Scallop Sauce.

♥ ♥ ♥

FISH QUENELLES WITH APPLE CELERY SAUCE

Quenelle mixture is best made just before serving. Sauce can be made a day ahead.

1 cup dry white wine
½ cup water
1 bay leaf
1 onion, quartered

QUENELLES
½lb white fish fillets
2 egg whites
3 tablespoons lowfat plain yogurt
4 teaspoons fresh lemon juice

APPLE CELERY SAUCE
1 stalk celery, chopped
1 onion, chopped
1 apple, chopped
4 teaspoons fresh lemon juice
¾ cup water
1 green onion, chopped
4 teaspoons chopped fresh chives

Combine wine, water, bay leaf and onion in pan, bring to boil, simmer, uncovered, 5 minutes, strain; discard onion and bay leaf. Return liquid to pan, simmer.

Mold quenelle mixture into oval shapes using 2 wet teaspoons. Spoon ovals into simmering liquid, poach, about 1 minute on each side. Do not allow water to come to the boil or quenelles will fall apart. Drain quenelles on absorbent paper, serve with apple celery sauce.

Quenelles: Blend or process fish, egg whites, yogurt and juice until smooth.
Apple Celery Sauce: Combine celery, onion, apple, juice and water in pan, bring to boil, simmer, covered, about 10 minutes or until vegetables are soft. Stir in onion; cool slightly. Blend or process mixture until smooth; stir in chives.

Serves 2.

- Not suitable to freeze.
- Not suitable to microwave.
  Total fat: 4.5 grams.
- Fat per serve: 2.3 grams.

BELOW: Clockwise from front: Salmon and Herb Souffles, Fish Quenelles with Apple Celery Sauce, Hearty Oyster Soup.

HERBED MUSSELS AND FISH

Cook recipe just before serving.

12 large mussels
2 teaspoons olive oil
1 onion, sliced
1 clove garlic, minced
1 stalk celery, chopped
14½oz can no-added-salt tomatoes
**4 teaspoons no-added-salt
   tomato paste**
¼ cup dry white wine
½ cup water
1 teaspoon chopped fresh thyme
10oz white fish fillets, chopped
2 teaspoons chopped fresh parsley

Remove beards from mussels, scrub shells. Heat oil in pan, add onion and garlic, cover, cook until soft. Add celery, undrained crushed tomatoes, paste, wine, water and thyme. Bring to boil, boil 2 minutes. Add mussels and fish, stir gently, simmer, covered, about 5 minutes or until seafood is just cooked. Serve sprinkled with parsley.

Serves 2.

- Not suitable to freeze.
- Not suitable to microwave.
  Total fat: 16.9 grams.
- Fat per serve: 8.5 grams.

FISH KABOBS WITH CHILI SAUCE

Recipe can be prepared a day ahead.

10½oz white fish fillets, chopped
**4 teaspoons reduced sodium
   soy sauce**
1 clove garlic, minced
¼ teaspoon grated fresh gingerroot
1 red bell pepper, chopped
1 green bell pepper, chopped
2 teaspoons olive oil
1 cup cooked rice

CHILI SAUCE
1 small fresh red chili pepper
2 cloves garlic, minced
4 teaspoons chopped fresh cilantro
4 teaspoons fish sauce
4 teaspoons fresh lime juice
2 tablespoons dark brown sugar
1 teaspoon olive oil
2 teaspoons cornstarch
4 teaspoons mirin
¾ cup water

Combine fish with sauce, garlic and gingerroot in bowl; refrigerate 1 hour. Thread fish and peppers alternately onto 4 skewers. Brush with oil, cook under heated broiler until fish is just cooked. Serve on rice with sauce.

Chili Sauce: Grind chopped chili, garlic and cilantro to smooth paste. Add sauce, juice and sugar. Heat oil in pan, add chili mixture, stir until sugar is dissolved; stir in blended cornstarch and mirin with water, stir until sauce boils and thickens.

Serves 2.

- Not suitable to freeze.
- Not suitable to microwave.
  Total fat: 17.2 grams.
- Fat per serve: 8.6 grams.

*ABOVE: Herbed Mussels and Fish.
RIGHT: From top: Fish Kabobs with Chili Sauce, Curried Fish Crumble, Rolled Fish Fillets with Mushroom Sauce.*

CURRIED FISH CRUMBLE

Recipe can be made 3 hours ahead.

¾lb mullet fillets
1 teaspoon olive oil
1 onion, chopped
1 bunch (1¼lb) spinach, shredded
1 carrot, sliced
1 parsnip, sliced
4 teaspoons cornstarch
1 cup skim milk
½ vegetable bouillon cube, crumbled
1 teaspoon curry powder

CRUMBLE TOPPING
¼ cup old-fashioned oats
¼ cup grated Parmesan cheese
3 tablespoons whole-wheat flour
2 teaspoons polyunsaturated
   margarine
4 teaspoons chopped fresh chives

Place fish in pan, cover with water, bring to boil, simmer, uncovered, about 3 minutes or until fish is just cooked. Drain, remove and discard skin, flake fish into bowl.

Heat oil in pan, add onion, cook until soft. Add spinach, cook, stirring, until spinach is wilted. Spoon spinach mixture into 2 ovenproof dishes (2 cup capacity).

Boil, steam or microwave carrot and parsnip until tender, place on top of spinach, then top with fish.

Blend cornstarch with milk in pan, stir in bouillon cube and curry powder. Stir over heat until sauce boils and thickens; pour over fish. Sprinkle topping over sauce, bake in 350°F oven about 30 minutes or until heated through and lightly browned.
Crumble Topping: Combine oats, cheese and flour in bowl, rub in margarine; stir in chives.

Serves 2.

- Not suitable to freeze.
- Not suitable to microwave.
- Total fat: 24.7 grams.
- Fat per serve: 12.4 grams.

ROLLED FISH FILLETS WITH MUSHROOM SAUCE

Make recipe close to serving time.

6 x 2½oz white fish fillets
2 teaspoons fresh lemon juice

MUSHROOM SAUCE
2 teaspoons olive oil
2 teaspoons all-purpose flour
¾ cup skim milk
¼ cup water
½ small chicken bouillon
   cube, crumbled
3 green onions, chopped
2oz small mushrooms, sliced
4 teaspoons dry white wine
1 teaspoon fresh lemon juice
¼ teaspoon dried thyme leaves
2 teaspoons light sour cream

Roll fish fillets, secure with toothpicks, drizzle with juice. Steam about 5 minutes or until just cooked. Serve with sauce.
Mushroom Sauce: Heat oil in pan, stir in flour, cook until bubbling. Remove from heat, gradually stir in combined milk, water and bouillon cube, onions, mushrooms, wine, juice and thyme, stir over heat until mixture boils and thickens, stir in sour cream.

Serves 2.

- Not suitable to freeze.
- Suitable to microwave.
- Total fat: 18.5 grams.
- Fat per serve: 9.2 grams.

Poultry

♥ ♥ ♥
ROLLED TURKEY WITH NUTTY SPINACH SEASONING

Recipe can be made a day ahead.

14oz turkey breast fillet

NUTTY SPINACH SEASONING
¼ cup cooked rice
1 large spinach leaf, chopped
2 green onions, chopped
4 teaspoons chopped roasted hazelnuts
1 teaspoon grated lemon zest
1 teaspoon chopped fresh thyme
1 egg white

CRANBERRY SAUCE
3 tablespoons cranberry sauce
1 teaspoon brandy
½ teaspoon grated orange zest
3 tablespoons water

Remove skin from turkey, pound turkey until thin, spread evenly with seasoning, roll turkey from short end, secure with kitchen string at 1 inch intervals.

Place turkey in oven bag, bake in 350°F oven about 40 minutes or until cooked through. Remove turkey from oven bag, cool; remove string. Cut into slices, serve cold with sauce.
Nutty Spinach Seasoning: Combine all ingredients in bowl.
Cranberry Sauce: Strain sauce into bowl, stir in remaining ingredients.

Serves 4.

- Not suitable to freeze.
- Suitable to microwave.
- Total fat: 12.4 grams.
- Fat per serve: 3.1 grams.

♥ ♥ ♥
MINTED TURKEY SLICE

Recipe is best made a day ahead.

2 small green cucumbers, sliced
2 teaspoons unflavored gelatin
4 teaspoons water
7oz piece boneless cooked turkey breast
½ red bell pepper, finely chopped
3 tablespoons chopped fresh mint
3 tablespoons dry sherry
14oz can chicken consomme
4 teaspoons chopped fresh chives
4 teaspoons unflavored gelatin, extra
¼ cup water, extra

Arrange cucumber slices along center of 3 inch x 10½ inch baking pan.

Sprinkle gelatin over water in cup, stand in small pan of simmering water, stir until dissolved; pour evenly over cucumbers. Refrigerate until set.

Chop turkey into ½ inch cubes. Combine turkey, pepper, mint, sherry, consomme and chives in bowl.

Sprinkle extra gelatin over extra water in cup, stand in small pan of simmering water, stir until dissolved; cool slightly. stir extra gelatin mixture into turkey mixture, pour mixture into pan; refrigerate until set.

Serves 2.

- Not suitable to freeze.
- Not suitable to microwave.
- Total fat: 5.4 grams.
- Fat per serve: 2.7 grams.

RIGHT: From left: Minted Turkey Slice, Rolled Turkey with Nutty Spinach Seasoning.

Blend or process chicken, cheese, cinnamon and parsley until mixture is almost smooth. Place a teaspoon of mixture onto center of each pastry sheet, brush edges with water, gather edges together to form pouches. Add dumplings to large pan of boiling water, simmer, uncovered, about 8 minutes or until cooked through, drain. Serve with spinach and raisins.

Spinach and Raisins: Combine spinach, pepper and carrot in nonstick skillet, cook, covered, until pepper is soft. Stir in raisins, juice, almonds and buttermilk, stir until heated through.

Serves 2.

- ■ Not suitable to freeze.
- ■ Suitable to microwave.
- Total fat: 22 grams.
- ■ Fat per serve: 11 grams.

♥
CORNMEAL DRUMSTICKS WITH CURRY SAUCE

Make recipe just before serving.

4 chicken drumsticks
3 egg whites, lightly beaten
1 cup (7oz) yellow cornmeal

CURRY SAUCE
½ cup skim milk
1 onion, finely chopped
1 teaspoon ground cumin
½ teaspoon ground coriander
1 teaspoon garam masala
½ teaspoon ground black pepper
1 teaspoon sugar
1 clove garlic, minced
1 small fresh red chili pepper, chopped
4 teaspoons cornstarch
4 teaspoons skim milk, extra

Remove skin from drumsticks, dip drumsticks into egg whites, roll in cornmeal, place onto nonstick baking sheet. Bake in 350°F oven about 45 minutes or until cooked through. Serve with curry sauce.

Curry Sauce: Combine milk, onion, spices, sugar, garlic and chili in pan, bring to boil, boil 1 minute. Stir in blended cornstarch and extra milk, stir until sauce boils and thickens. Blend or process sauce until smooth.

Serves 2.

- ■ Not suitable to freeze.
- ■ Not suitable to microwave.
- Total fat: 25.3 grams.
- ■ Fat per serve: 12.7 grams.

♥ ♥ ♥
CHICKEN AND ARTICHOKE PIES

Make recipe just before serving.

4 teaspoons dry white wine
½ cup water
1 stalk celery, chopped
2 teaspoons chopped fresh oregano
1 onion, chopped
½ small chicken bouillon cube, crumbled
4 teaspoons all-purpose flour
½ cup skim milk
¾lb boneless, skinless chicken breast halves, chopped
13oz can artichokes in brine, drained, chopped
2 sheets phyllo pastry

Combine wine, water, celery, oregano, onion and bouillon cube in pan, bring to boil, simmer, uncovered, until onion is soft. Stir in blended flour and milk, stir until mixture boils and thickens. Stir in chicken and artichokes, simmer uncovered, about 5 minutes or until chicken is cooked through. Spoon mixture into 2 ovenproof dishes (1½ cup capacity).

Cut 1 pastry sheet lengthways into quarters, cut remaining sheet crossways into 8. Roll strips of pastry, gathering on 1 edge, to form roses, trim, arrange roses on top of each pie. Place pies on baking sheet, bake in 375°F oven about 15 minutes or until pastry is lightly browned and crisp.

Serves 2.

- ■ Not suitable to freeze.
- ■ Not suitable to microwave.
- Total fat: 8.6 grams.
- ■ Fat per serve: 4.3 grams.

♥
CHICKEN DUMPLINGS WITH SPINACH AND RAISINS

Dumplings can be made a day ahead.

½lb chicken thighs, boned, skinned, chopped
1½oz reduced fat feta cheese, mashed
¼ teaspoon ground cinnamon
3 tablespoons chopped fresh parsley
3½oz package 3in round gow gees pastry

SPINACH AND RAISINS
½ bunch (10oz) spinach, shredded
1 red bell pepper, sliced
1 carrot, chopped
¼ cup golden raisins
4 teaspoons fresh lemon juice
4 teaspoons sliced almonds
⅓ cup buttermilk

ABOVE: Chicken and Artichoke Pies.
RIGHT: From top: Cornmeal Drumsticks with Curry Sauce, Chicken Dumplings with Spinach and Raisins.

♥ ♥ BROILED TANDOORI CHICKEN

Recipe can be prepared a day ahead.

½ cup lowfat plain yogurt
4 teaspoons fresh lemon juice
½ teaspoon grated fresh gingerroot
1 clove garlic, minced
½ teaspoon granulated sugar
½ teaspoon paprika
¼ teaspoon ground cumin
¼ teaspoon ground coriander
¼ teaspoon turmeric
⅛ teaspoon chili powder
2 x 7oz boneless, skinless chicken
    breast halves

Combine yogurt, juice, gingerroot, garlic, sugar and spices in bowl. Add chicken, turn chicken to coat in marinade; refrigerate several hours or overnight. Broil chicken, brushing with marinade, until browned and cooked through.

Serves 2.

■ Not suitable to freeze.
■ Not suitable to microwave.
  Total fat: 9.2 grams.
■ Fat per serve: 4.6 grams.

♥ ♥ ♥ SMOKED CHICKEN WITH SHERRY SAUCE

Sauce can be made 2 days ahead.
Cook chicken just before serving.

½ cup Chinese assorted spices
¼ cup sugar
3 tablespoons black peppercorns
¼ cup uncooked rice
2 x 5oz boneless, skinless chicken
    breast halves
1 cup cooked rice

SHERRY SAUCE
¼ cup dry sherry
¼ cup water
1 teaspoon sugar
1 teaspoon chopped fresh gingerroot
1½ teaspoons cornstarch
2 tablespoons reduced sodium
    soy sauce
1 green onion, sliced

Line wok with foil. Combine spices, sugar, peppercorns and uncooked rice in wok. Place a rack in wok above spice mixture. Place chicken on rack, cover wok with tight lid, cook over medium heat about 25 minutes or until chicken is cooked through. Serve sliced chicken with sherry sauce and cooked rice.

Sherry Sauce: Combine sherry, water, sugar and gingerroot in pan, stir in blended cornstarch and sauce. Stir over heat until mixture boils and thickens, stir in onion; mix well.

Serves 2.

■ Not suitable to freeze.
■ Not suitable to microwave.
  Total fat: 7 grams.
■ Fat per serve: 3.5 grams.

♥
CHICKEN LOAF WITH TOMATO CHILI SAUCE

Loaf can be made 3 hours ahead.
Sauce can be made a day ahead.

7oz boneless, skinless chicken
breast halves, chopped
2 teaspoons olive oil
¼ small leek, sliced
½ small red bell pepper, sliced
2 teaspoons all-purpose flour
⅓ cup skim milk
¼ cup fresh white bread crumbs
4 teaspoons grated Parmesan cheese
1 egg white, lightly beaten
4 teaspoons chopped fresh tarragon

TOMATO CHILI SAUCE
1 teaspoon olive oil
½ small onion, chopped
1 small tomato, peeled, chopped
1 small fresh red chili pepper,
chopped
1 teaspoon no-added-salt
tomato paste
1 teaspoon fresh lemon juice

Lightly grease 2 small loaf pans (¾ cup capacity), line base with paper, lightly grease paper.

Blend or process chicken until finely chopped. Heat oil in pan, add leek and pepper, cook until leek is soft, stir in flour, cook 1 minute. Remove from heat, gradually stir in milk, stir over heat until mixture boils and thickens.

Combine leek mixture with chicken and remaining ingredients in bowl. Spoon mixture into prepared pans, place pans in roasting pan, pour in enough boiling water to come halfway up sides of loaf pans. Bake in 350°F oven about 25 minutes before turning onto wire rack to cool. Serve with tomato chili sauce.

Tomato Chili Sauce: Heat oil in skillet, add onion, cook, stirring, until soft. Stir in remaining ingredients, simmer, uncovered, 2 minutes; cool.

Serves 2.

■ Not suitable to freeze.
■ Not suitable to microwave.
☐ Total fat: 21.3 grams.
■ Fat per serve: 10.6 grams.

♥ ♥ ♥
BRANDIED TURKEY PATE

Pate can be made 2 days ahead.

1 whole-wheat pita bread round
7oz piece boneless, skinless turkey
breast half, chopped
1 onion, chopped
1 eggplant, chopped
4 teaspoons whole-wheat flour
4 teaspoons chopped fresh basil
½ cup water
3 tablespoons brandy
4 teaspoons drained green
peppercorns
2 teaspoons unflavored gelatin
¼ cup water, extra

Cut bread into 8 wedges, place on baking sheet, bake in 350°F oven about 15 minutes or until crisp.

Combine turkey, onion and eggplant in nonstick skillet, stir over heat until well browned. Stir in flour, cook 3 minutes. Stir in basil and water, bring to boil; cool.

Blend or process turkey mixture and brandy until almost smooth. Stir in peppercorns. Spoon mixture into mold (2 cup capacity). Sprinkle unflavored gelatin over extra water in cup, stand in small pan of simmering water, stir until dissolved. Pour over pate, decorate with herbs, if desired; refrigerate until set. Serve pate with pita bread wedges.

Serves 2.

■ Not suitable to freeze.
■ Suitable to microwave.
☐ Total fat: 5.8 grams.
■ Fat per serve: 2.9 grams.

ABOVE LEFT: From top: Broiled Tandoori Chicken, Smoked Chicken with Sherry Sauce.
ABOVE RIGHT: From top: Chicken Loaf with Tomato Chili Sauce, Brandied Turkey Pate.

♥ BROILED QUAIL WITH RED CURRANT SAUCE

Cook quail just before serving.

4 quail
2 cups dry white wine
¼ cup white wine vinegar
4 black peppercorns
1 clove
1 bay leaf
1 small carrot, chopped
½ stalk celery, chopped
1 small onion, chopped
2 parsley sprigs, chopped
1 teaspoon olive oil

RED CURRANT SAUCE
3 tablespoons red currant jelly
1 teaspoon cornstarch
1 tablespoon water
**3 tablespoons fresh or frozen
   red currants**

Using scissors, cut down both sides of backbone of each quail. Remove and discard backbones. Using heel of hand, press quail flat. Trim wings to second joint, remove skin and any visible fat from quail. Place quail in single layer in shallow dish.

Combine wine, vinegar, peppercorns, clove, bay leaf, carrot, celery, onion and parsley in bowl; pour over quail; refrigerate 2 hours. Remove quail from marinade; reserve marinade. Pat quail dry with absorbent paper, brush with oil, broil until lightly browned and cooked through. Serve with sauce.

Red Currant Sauce: Place reserved marinade in pan, bring to boil, simmer, uncovered, 3 minutes. Remove from heat, strain; return 1 cup of liquid to pan. Bring to boil, boil until reduced by half. Add jelly, stir until dissolved. Stir in blended cornstarch and water, stir until mixture boils and thickens; stir in red currants.

Serves 2.

■ Not suitable to freeze.
■ Not suitable to microwave.
   Total fat: 22 grams.
■ Fat per serve: 11 grams.

♥ ♥ GINGERROOT CHICKEN KABOBS

Cook recipe just before serving.

**10oz boneless, skinless chicken
   breast halves, chopped**
4 teaspoons green ginger wine
**4 teaspoons reduced sodium
   soy sauce**
4 teaspoons fresh lemon juice
1 teaspoon olive oil
2 teaspoons Worcestershire sauce
2 teaspoons dark brown sugar
½ teaspoon dry mustard
1 teaspoon grated fresh gingerroot

Combine chicken and remaining ingredients in bowl, refrigerate several hours. Thread chicken onto skewers, reserve marinade. Broil kabobs, occasionally brushing with marinade, until chicken is cooked through.

Serves 2.

■ Not suitable to freeze.
■ Suitable to microwave.
   Total fat: 11.4 grams.
■ Fat per serve: 5.7 grams.

♥ ♥ ♥ FRUITY CHICKEN CURRY

Recipe can be made a day ahead.

1 teaspoon olive oil
1 onion, chopped
1 teaspoon ground cumin
1 teaspoon curry powder
14½oz can no-added-salt tomatoes
¼ cup chutney
3 tablespoons honey
4 teaspoons white vinegar
**7oz boneless, skinless chicken
   breast halves, chopped**
2 bananas, chopped

Heat oil in pan, add onion, cumin, curry powder and juice from tomatoes, cook until onion is soft. Add undrained crushed tomatoes, chutney, honey and vinegar, bring to boil, simmer, uncovered, about 5 minutes or until mixture is thick. Stir in chopped chicken and bananas, simmer, uncovered, about 5 minutes or until chicken is cooked through.

Serves 2.

■ Not suitable to freeze.
■ Suitable to microwave.
   Total fat: 9 grams.
■ Fat per serve: 4.5 grams.

LEFT: Clockwise from front: Gingerroot Chicken Kabobs, Fruity Chicken Curry, Broiled Quail with Red Currant Sauce.

Rabbit

♥ ♥ ♥
RABBIT AND TOMATO VEGETABLE CASSEROLE

Make casserole just before serving.

15oz rabbit pieces
½ cup fresh or frozen green peas
7oz pumpkin squash, chopped
½ red bell pepper, chopped
1 large onion, chopped
15oz can tomato puree
1 clove garlic, minced
½ cup dry white wine
3 tablespoons chopped fresh parsley
½ cup water

Combine all ingredients in pan, bring to boil, simmer, covered, about 1¼ hours or until rabbit is tender.

Serves 2.

■ Suitable to freeze.
■ Suitable to microwave.
   Total fat: 9.2 grams.
■ Fat per serve: 4.6 grams.

♥ ♥
SWEET AND SOUR BAKED RABBIT

Make recipe just before serving.

1 teaspoon olive oil
15oz rabbit pieces
3 tablespoons no-added-salt tomato ketchup
4 teaspoons cider vinegar
½ teaspoon sugar
4 teaspoons all-purpose flour
1 small green bell pepper, chopped
7½oz drained canned pineapple chunks
4 teaspoons chopped fresh parsley

Heat oil in nonstick skillet, add rabbit, cook until browned all over. Drain rabbit on absorbent paper; place in oven bag.
   Combine ketchup, vinegar, sugar and flour in bowl; stir in remaining ingredients. Pour mixture over rabbit in bag, seal bag, pierce bag several times near sealed end,

place bag in roasting pan, bake in 350˚F oven about 1¼ hours or until tender.

Serves 2.

■ Not suitable to freeze.
■ Not suitable to microwave.
   Total fat: 13.7 grams.
■ Fat per serve: 6.9 grams.

ABOVE: Rabbit and Tomato Vegetable Casserole.
RIGHT: From top: Sweet and Sour Baked Rabbit, Hearty Rabbit Stew.

♥ ♥
HEARTY RABBIT STEW

Cook recipe close to serving time.

14oz rabbit pieces
4 teaspoons all-purpose flour
1 teaspoon olive oil
¾ cup water
½ cup dry white wine
2 teaspoons no-added-salt
   tomato paste
½ small chicken bouillon
   cube, crumbled
1 carrot, chopped
1 potato, chopped
4 pearl onions
½ cup frozen green peas

Toss rabbit in flour, shake away excess flour. Heat oil in pan, add rabbit, cook until rabbit is browned all over. Stir in water, wine, paste and bouillon cube, bring to boil, simmer, covered, 1 hour. Add carrot, potato and onions, cook 15 minutes, add peas, cook until vegetables are tender.

Serves 2.

■ Not suitable to freeze.
■ Not suitable to microwave.
  Total fat: 12.5 grams.
■ Fat per serve: 6.3 grams.

Vegetarian

HERBED RATATOUILLE WITH PASTA

Sauce can be made a day ahead.

1 teaspoon olive oil
1 clove garlic, minced
1 onion, chopped
1 eggplant, chopped
4 zucchini, chopped
1 green bell pepper, chopped
2 tomatoes, chopped
4 teaspoons dry red wine
4 teaspoons no-added-salt
   tomato paste
4 teaspoons chopped fresh basil
10oz pasta

Heat oil in nonstick skillet, add garlic and onion, cook until soft. Stir in eggplant, cook until eggplant is soft, remove from skillet; drain on absorbent paper. Cook zucchini and bell pepper separately, following same method as eggplant. Return vegetables with tomatoes, wine, pasta and basil to skillet, cook 5 minutes or until mixture is heated through.

Add pasta to large pan of boiling water, boil, uncovered, until just tender; drain. Serve with ratatouille.

Serves 2.

■ Not suitable to freeze.
■ Suitable to microwave.
□ Total fat: 8.4 grams.
■ Fat per serve: 4.2 grams.

♥ ♥

SPINACH MARJORAM CREPES

Crepes can be made 2 days ahead.
Sauce can be made a day ahead.
Assemble crepes just before serving.

1 bunch (1¼lb) spinach
¼lb reduced fat ricotta cheese
3 tablespoons grated Parmesan
   cheese
1 teaspoon chopped fresh marjoram

CREPES
¼ cup all-purpose flour
1 egg white
⅓ cup skim milk

SAUCE
½ cup skim milk
2 teaspoons no-added-salt
   tomato paste
¼ small chicken bouillon
   cube, crumbled
1 bay leaf
1 teaspoon all-purpose flour
1 teaspoon olive oil

Boil, steam or microwave spinach until tender; drain on absorbent paper, cool; chop roughly.

Combine spinach, cheeses and marjoram in bowl. Spread crepes with spinach mixture, roll crepes, place in ovenproof dish. Cover, bake in 350°F oven about 20 minutes or until heated through. Serve crepes with sauce.

Crepes: Sift flour into bowl, gradually stir in combined egg white and milk to make a smooth batter.

Pour quarter of the batter into heated nonstick crepe pan, cook until lightly browned underneath. Turn crepe, brown on other side. Repeat with remaining crepe batter.

Sauce: Combine milk, paste, bouillon cube and bay leaf in pan, bring to boil, stir in combined flour and oil. Stir until sauce boils and thickens, strain; discard bay leaf.

Serves 2.

■ Not suitable to freeze.
■ Not suitable to microwave.
□ Total fat: 16.9 grams.
■ Fat per serve: 8.5 grams.

VEGETARIAN PIZZA

Pizza can be prepared 3 hours ahead.

1 package (¼oz) active dry yeast
½ teaspoon sugar
½ cup water
1½ cups all-purpose flour
1 teaspoon olive oil
¼ cup no-added-salt tomato paste
½ cup canned drained kidney beans
1 small onion, sliced
1 small zucchini, sliced
1 small red bell pepper, sliced
4 button mushrooms, sliced
¾ cup bean sprouts
¼ teaspoon dried basil leaves
¼ teaspoon dried oregano leaves
¼ cup shredded reduced fat
   mozzarella cheese
4 teaspoons grated Parmesan cheese

Combine yeast with sugar in bowl, stir in water. Cover, stand in warm place about 10 minutes or until mixture is frothy. Sift flour into bowl, stir in yeast mixture and oil, mix to firm dough.

Turn dough onto floured surface, knead about 5 minutes or until dough is smooth and elastic.

Return dough to bowl, cover, stand in warm place about 45 minutes or until doubled in size. Turn dough onto lightly floured surface, knead until smooth.

Roll dough large enough to line 8 inch round pizza pan. Spread dough with paste, top with remaining ingredients. Bake in 375°F oven about 25 minutes or until crust is crisp.

Serves 2.

■ Suitable to freeze.
■ Not suitable of microwave.
□ Total fat: 15.1 grams.
■ Fat per serve: 7.6 grams.

Left: Clockwise from front: Spinach Marjoram Crepes; Herbed Ratatouille with Pasta, Vegetarian Pizza.

VEGETABLE RISOTTO

Risotto can be made 3 hours ahead.

1 small eggplant, chopped
coarse (kosher) salt
2 teaspoons olive oil
1 small onion, chopped
1 clove garlic, minced
¾ cup brown rice
½ small chicken bouillon
   cube, crumbled
2¾ cups water
1 eggplant, chopped
1 small red bell pepper, chopped
2 tomatoes, peeled, chopped
2 zucchini, thinly sliced
¼lb mushrooms, sliced
2 teaspoons chopped fresh oregano
¼ cup grated Parmesan cheese

Place eggplant in colander, sprinkle with salt, stand 30 minutes. Rinse well under cold water, pat dry with absorbent paper.

Heat oil in pan, add onion and garlic, cook until soft. Add rice, bouillon cube and water, bring to boil, simmer, covered, about 30 minutes or until rice is tender and almost all the liquid is absorbed.

Stir in eggplant, pepper, tomatoes, zucchini, mushrooms and oregano; cook about 3 minutes or until vegetables are soft. Stir in half the cheese, serve risotto sprinkled with remaining cheese.

Serves 2.

■ Not suitable to freeze.
■ Suitable to microwave.
  Total fat: 21.6 grams.
■ Fat per serve: 10.8 grams.

♥ ♥
ZUCCHINI LENTIL PASTIES WITH SPICY CHILI SAUCE

Recipe can be made 3 hours ahead.

1 onion, chopped
2 cloves garlic, minced
1 teaspoon curry powder
½ teaspoon grated fresh gingerroot
¼ teaspoon sambal oelek
¼ cup red lentils
⅔ cup water
1 zucchini, grated
1½ sheets (5½oz) ready rolled
   whole-wheat pastry
1 egg white

SPICY CHILI SAUCE
½ cup white vinegar
3 tablespoons sweet sherry
2 teaspoons reduced sodium
   soy sauce
½ teaspoon sambal oelek
1 teaspoon cornstarch
2 teaspoons water
2 teaspoons chopped fresh parsley

Cook onion, garlic, curry powder, gingerroot and sambal oelek in nonstick pan 1 minute, stir in lentils and water. Bring to boil, simmer, uncovered, about 10 minutes or until all liquid is absorbed. Remove from heat, stir in zucchini.

Cut 6 rounds from pastry using 5 inch cutter. Divide filling between rounds, fold rounds to enclose filling; pinch edges together to seal. Brush with egg white, place on paper-covered baking sheet, bake in 375°F oven about 25 minutes or until well browned. Serve with sauce.

Spicy Chili Sauce: Combine vinegar, sherry, sauce and sambal oelek in pan, stir in blended cornstarch and water. Stir over heat until sauce boils and thickens. Stir in parsley.

Makes 6.

■ Not suitable to freeze.
■ Not suitable to microwave.
  Total fat: 39 grams.
■ Fat per pasty: 6.5 grams.

♥
TEMPEH VEGETABLE BASKETS

*We used 6 inch square egg roll skins.
Baskets can be made 3 hours ahead.
Filling best cooked just before serving.*

4 egg roll skins
1 egg white

VEGETABLE FILLING
4 teaspoons no-added-salt
   peanut butter
3 tablespoons reduced sodium
   soy sauce
7oz tempeh, chopped
2 teaspoons olive oil
1 onion, chopped
1 clove garlic, minced
¾ cup canned sliced bamboo
   shoots, rinsed, drained
1 red bell pepper, sliced
½ Chinese cabbage, shredded
2 green onions, sliced
3 tablespoons green ginger wine
4 teaspoons reduced sodium soy
   sauce, extra
1 teaspoon cornstarch
¼ cup water

Wet 2 x 12 inch squares baking paper, wrap around base and side of 2 inverted souffle dishes (1 cup capacity); place dishes onto baking sheet.

Brush egg roll skins lightly with egg white, layer 2 skins at an angle, place over prepared dish, shape skins around dish. Repeat with remaining dish and skins.

Bake baskets in 350°F oven about 8 minutes or until lightly browned. Remove baskets from dishes, add filling just before serving.

Vegetable Filling: Combine peanut butter and sauce in bowl, stir in tempeh, stand several hours.

Heat oil in wok or skillet, add tempeh mixture, stir-fry until lightly browned,

remove from wok. Add onion, garlic, bamboo shoots and pepper to wok, stir-fry 1 minute. Add cabbage and onions, stir-fry until just wilted. Stir in tempeh mixture, wine, extra sauce and blended

cornstarch and water, stir until mixture boils and thickens.

Serves 2.

■ Not suitable to freeze.
■ Not suitable to microwave.
□ Total fat: 27.4 grams.
■ Fat per serve: 13.7 grams.

ABOVE: Clockwise from back: Tempeh Vegetable Baskets, Zucchini Lentil Pasties with Spicy Chili Sauce, Vegetable Risotto.

♥ ♥
MINTED VEGETABLE TERRINE
Recipe is best prepared a day ahead.

7oz reduced fat ricotta cheese
½ cup lowfat plain yogurt
2 teaspoons grated lemon zest
3 tablespoons chopped fresh mint
4 teaspoons chopped fresh parsley
1 small green cucumber, chopped
1½oz mushrooms, chopped
1 small carrot, chopped
1 clove garlic, minced
1 tablespoon unflavored gelatin
¼ cup water

Rinse 3 inch x 10½ inch baking pan in cold water. Beat cheese and yogurt in bowl with electric mixer until smooth and creamy. Stir in zest, herbs, cucumber, mushrooms, carrot and garlic.

Sprinkle gelatin over water in cup, stand in small pan of simmering water, stir until dissolved; cool slightly. Stir gelatin mixture into vegetable mixture, spoon into prepared pan, refrigerate overnight.

Serves 2.

- ◼ Not suitable to freeze.
- ◼ Not suitable to microwave.
- ◻ Total fat: 17 grams.
- ◼ Fat per serve: 8.5 grams.

♥ ♥
HOT VEGETABLE AND TOFU SALAD
Make recipe just before serving.

2 teaspoons olive oil
1 onion, quartered
1 teaspoon grated fresh gingerroot
½lb package firm tofu, chopped
1 small carrot, sliced
1 small red bell pepper, sliced
3½oz broccoli, chopped
3½oz snow peas
1 stalk celery, sliced
½ cup water
½ vegetable bouillon cube, crumbled
3 tablespoons oyster-flavored sauce
4 teaspoons reduced sodium soy sauce

Heat oil in pan, add onion and gingerroot, cook until onion is soft. Stir in tofu and remaining ingredients, bring to boil, simmer, uncovered, about 5 minutes or until vegetables are tender.

Serves 2.

- ◼ Not suitable to freeze.
- ◼ Suitable to microwave.
- ◻ Total fat: 19.5 grams.
- ◼ Fat per serve: 9.7 grams.

♥ ♥
VEGETABLE PARCELS WITH PUMPKIN SQUASH SAUCE
Parcels can be prepared 3 hours ahead. Sauce can be made a day ahead.

2 teaspoons olive oil
1 small leek, chopped
1 carrot, chopped
1 small red bell pepper, chopped
1 stalk celery, chopped
3½oz mushrooms, chopped
½ cup frozen green peas
3 tablespoons chopped fresh parsley
3 tablespoons chopped fresh basil
4 teaspoons no-added-salt tomato paste
4 egg roll skins
1 egg white, lightly beaten
1 tablespoon grated Parmesan cheese

PUMPKIN SQUASH SAUCE
5oz pumpkin squash, chopped
1 small onion, chopped
1 cup water
½ vegetable bouillon cube, crumbled
2 teaspoons no-added-salt tomato paste

Heat oil in pan, add leek, carrot, pepper and celery, cover, cook about 15 minutes or until leek is soft. Stir in mushrooms, peas, herbs and paste, cook 5 minutes; cool to room temperature.

Place quarter of the leek mixture along 1 side of an egg roll skin, fold in sides and roll up like a jelly-roll. Repeat with remaining leek mixture and skins. Place parcels on baking paper-covered baking sheet, brush with egg white, sprinkle with cheese. Bake in 350°F oven about 30 minutes or until lightly browned. Serve with sauce.

Pumpkin Squash Sauce: Combine all ingredients in pan, bring to boil, simmer, covered, about 15 minutes or until squash is soft. Blend or process squash mixture until smooth. Reheat if necessary.

Serves 2.

- ◼ Not suitable to freeze.
- ◼ Not suitable to microwave.
- ◻ Total fat: 12.2 grams.
- ◼ Fat per serve: 6.1 grams.

RIGHT: Clockwise from back: Minted Vegetable Terrine, Hot Vegetable and Tofu Salad, Vegetable Parcels with Pumpkin Squash Sauce.

♥
VEGETABLE MOUSSAKA

Make recipe just before serving.

1 large eggplant, sliced
4 teaspoons all-purpose flour
½ cup buttermilk
½ cup skim milk
4 teaspoons nonfat dry milk
7 oz reduced fat ricotta cheese
3½oz no-cholesterol egg substitute,
  lightly beaten
4 teaspoons chopped fresh parsley
14½oz can no-added-salt tomatoes
4 teaspoons chopped fresh basil
1 teaspoon granulated sugar
¼ teaspoon paprika

Arrange eggplant in single layer on baking sheet. Bake in 375°F oven 30 minutes, turning eggplant after 15 minutes; cool.

Combine flour, milks, dry milk, cheese, egg substitute and parsley in small bowl. Combine undrained crushed tomatoes, basil and sugar in pan, bring to boil, simmer, uncovered, about 15 minutes or until mixture is thick.

Layer eggplant, cheese mixture and tomato mixture in ovenproof dish (4 cup capacity), finishing with cheese mixture. Sprinkle with paprika, bake in 350°F oven about 40 minutes or until mixture is set and lightly browned.

Serves 2.

■ Not suitable to freeze.
■ Not suitable to microwave.
  Total fat: 30.7 grams.
■ Fat per serve: 15.4 grams.

LEFT: Vegetable Moussaka.

Carrot and Potato Sauce: Combine all ingredients in pan, bring to boil, simmer, covered, about 20 minutes or until vegetables are soft. Discard bay leaf. Blend or process sauce mixture until smooth; strain.

Serves 2.

- ■ Not suitable to freeze.
- ■ Not suitable to microwave.
- ☐ Total fat: 5.8 grams.
- ■ Fat per serve: 2.9 grams.

♥

LENTIL PATTIES WITH YOGURT MINT SAUCE

Recipe can be made a day ahead.

½ cup red lentils
½ stalk celery, chopped
1 small carrot, chopped
2 cups water
½ teaspoon ground coriander
¼ teaspoon ground cumin
¼ teaspoon dried oregano leaves
4 teaspoons chopped fresh parsley
1 cup (2½oz) fresh bread crumbs
3 tablespoons all-purpose flour
1 egg white, lightly beaten
¼ cup packaged unseasoned
    bread crumbs
4 teaspoons olive oil

YOGURT MINT SAUCE
½ cup lowfat plain yogurt
2 teaspoons chopped fresh mint
2 teaspoons chopped fresh parsley
1 small clove garlic, minced
1 teaspoon lemon juice

Combine lentils, celery, carrot, water, coriander, cumin and oregano in pan. Bring to boil, simmer, covered, about 20 minutes or until mixture is thickened; cool. Stir in parsley and fresh bread crumbs. Shape mixture into 4 patties, toss in flour, dip in egg white, then packaged bread crumbs to coat.

    Heat oil in nonstick skillet, add patties, cook until well browned on both sides; drain on absorbent paper. Serve with yogurt mint sauce.

Yogurt Mint Sauce: Combine all ingredients in bowl; mix well.

Serves 2.

- ■ Patties suitable to freeze.
- ■ Not suitable to microwave.
- ☐ Total fat: 21.5 grams.
- ■ Fat per serve: 10.8 grams.

♥ ♥

ONION QUICHES

Make recipe just before serving.

2 teaspoons packaged unseasoned
    bread crumbs
1 teaspoon olive oil
3 onions, thinly sliced
1 teaspoon dark brown sugar
4 green onions, chopped
3 tablespoons chopped fresh chives
3½oz no-cholesterol egg substitute,
    lightly beaten
½ cup buttermilk
4 teaspoons all-purpose flour
1 egg white

Lightly grease 2 x 6 inch quiche dishes, sprinkle with bread crumbs.

    Heat oil in pan, add onions, cook until soft. Stir in sugar, cook further 10 minutes or until onions are very soft. Add green onions and chives; cool. Divide onion mixture between prepared dishes.

    Combine egg substitute, buttermilk and flour in bowl. Beat egg white in small bowl until soft peaks form, fold into buttermilk mixture; pour over onion mixture. Bake in 350°F oven about 35 minutes or until quiches are set and lightly browned.

Serves 2.

- ■ Not suitable to freeze.
- ■ Not suitable to microwave.
- ☐ Total fat: 15.2 grams.
- ■ Fat per serve: 7.6 grams.

♥ ♥ ♥

TOFU DUMPLINGS WITH CARROT AND POTATO SAUCE

Sauce can be made a day ahead.
Make dumplings just before serving.

TOFU DUMPLINGS
1 cup water
3 tablespoons self-rising flour
⅓ cup yellow cornmeal
½ teaspoon paprika
½ cup fresh bread crumbs
3½oz soft tofu, mashed
2 egg whites

CARROT AND POTATO SAUCE
1 carrot, chopped
3½oz sweet potato, chopped
¼ teaspoon cracked black
    peppercorns
½ onion, chopped
1 bay leaf
1½ cups water

Tofu Dumplings: Bring water to boil in pan, add combined flour, cornmeal and paprika all at once. Stir vigorously over heat until mixture is thick and leaves side of pan. Combine mixture with bread crumbs and tofu in bowl, beat with electric mixer until combined. Add egg whites, beat about 1 minute or until mixture is glossy; stand 10 minutes.

    Drop heaped teaspoons of mixture into pan of simmering water, cook 5 minutes or until cooked through; drain on absorbent paper. Serve dumplings with sauce.

ABOVE LEFT: Onion Quiches.
RIGHT: Clockwise from front: Tofu Dumplings with Carrot and Potato Sauce, Bean and Potato Bake, Lentil Patties with Yogurt Mint Sauce.

♥ ♥ ♥
BEAN AND POTATO BAKE

Make recipe just before serving.

4 (14oz) potatoes, thinly sliced
1 onion, thinly sliced
⅓ cup canned Mexicana chili beans
½ cup skim milk
¼ cup grated Parmesan cheese
½ teaspoon paprika

Layer potatoes, onion and beans in 2 lightly greased ovenproof dishes (1 cup capacity). Pour milk over vegetables, sprinkle with cheese and paprika. Bake, uncovered, in 350°F oven about 25 minutes or until vegetables are soft.

Serves 2.

☐ Not suitable to freeze.
■ Suitable to microwave.
☐ Total fat: 9.5 grams.
■ Fat per serve: 4.7 grams.

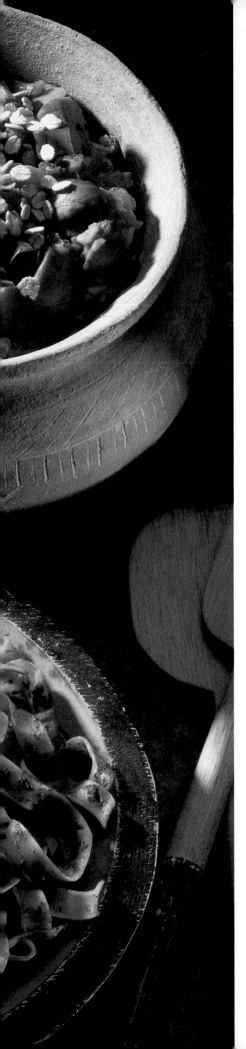

♥

TASTY VEGETABLE PIES

Pies can be prepared a day ahead.

4 teaspoons olive oil
1 small leek, sliced
3 tablespoons all-purpose flour
1 cup skim milk
1 zucchini, chopped
1 carrot, chopped
4 teaspoons chopped fresh parsley
½ sheet (10in x 10in) ready rolled
 whole-wheat pastry
½ teaspoon skim milk, extra
½ teaspoon grated Parmesan cheese

Heat oil in pan, stir in leek, cook until soft. Stir in flour, cook until bubbling. Remove from heat, gradually stir in milk, stir over heat until sauce boils and thickens; cover, cool to room temperature.

 Boil, steam or microwave zucchini and carrot until just tender. Stir vegetables and parsley into sauce. Spoon into 2 ovenproof dishes (1 cup capacity).

 Cut pastry into 2 rounds large enough to cover dishes, brush with extra milk, sprinkle with cheese. Bake in 375°F oven about 20 minutes or until pastry is lightly browned and crisp.

Serves 2.

■ Not suitable to freeze.
■ Not suitable to microwave.
 Total fat: 33.6 grams.
■ Fat per serve: 16.8 grams.

♥ ♥ ♥

RED RICE, BARLEY AND MUSHROOM CASSEROLES

Make recipe just before serving.

1 onion, sliced
7oz mushrooms, chopped
1 small leek, chopped
1 apple, chopped
3 tablespoons chopped fresh basil
1 tomato, chopped
⅓ cup red rice
14oz can chicken consomme
2 green onions, chopped
½ cup rolled barley
2 teaspoons rolled barley, extra

Combine onion, mushrooms, leek, apple, basil, tomato and rice in bowl. Spoon mixture into 2 ovenproof dishes (2 cup capacity). Divide consomme evenly between dishes, cover, cook in 350°F oven about 40 minutes or until rice is tender. Stir onions and barley into casseroles, cover, stand 5 minutes before serving. Serve sprinkled with extra barley.

Serves 2.

■ Not suitable to freeze.
■ Suitable to microwave.
 Total fat: 1.5 grams.
■ Fat per serve: Negligible.

♥

PASTA WITH PESTO SAUCE

Cook recipe just before serving.

2 cups fresh basil leaves
1 clove garlic, minced
⅓ cup grated Parmesan cheese
4 teaspoons olive oil
4 teaspoons no-oil French dressing
9oz pasta

Blend or process basil, garlic, cheese, oil and dressing until well combined.

 Add pasta to large pan of boiling water, boil, uncovered, until just tender; drain. Toss pesto through pasta before serving.

Serves 2.

■ Not suitable to freeze.
■ Not suitable to microwave.
 Total fat: 34.2 grams.
■ Fat per serve: 17.1 grams.

LEFT: Clockwise from front: Pasta with Pesto Sauce, Tasty Vegetable Pies, Red Rice, Barley and Mushroom Casseroles.

♥ ♥
SPICY BEAN CASSEROLE

Recipe can be made a day ahead.

½ cup dried red kidney beans
½ cup dried lima beans
2 teaspoons olive oil
1 red onion, sliced
1 carrot, sliced
1 small red bell pepper, chopped
1 clove garlic, minced
1 small fresh red chili, chopped
1 teaspoon ground cumin
½ teaspoon ground cinnamon
½ teaspoon ground nutmeg
14½oz can no-added-salt tomatoes
½ cup water
½ vegetable bouillon cube, crumbled
2 teaspoons no-added-salt
    tomato paste
2 teaspoons honey
½ cup canned no-added-salt whole
    kernel corn, drained

Cover beans with water in bowl, stand overnight; drain.

Heat oil in pan, add onion, carrot, pepper, garlic and chili, cook until onion is soft. Stir in cumin, cinnamon and nutmeg, cook further minute. Stir in beans, undrained crushed tomatoes, water, bouillon cube, paste and honey.

Bring to boil, simmer, covered, about 45 minutes, stirring occasionally, or until beans are tender. Stir in corn, simmer further 5 minutes.

Serves 2.

■ Not suitable to freeze.
■ Not suitable to microwave.
  Total fat: 13.5 grams.
■ Fat per serve: 6.8 grams.

♥ ♥ ♥
CURRIED VEGETABLE HOT POT

Curry can be made 3 hours ahead.

¼ cup water
1 teaspoon ground cumin
1 teaspoon ground coriander
1 teaspoon garam masala
1 teaspoon curry powder
14½oz can no-added-salt tomatoes
1¾ cups water, extra
2 potatoes, chopped
1 onion, chopped
2 carrots, chopped
1lb cauliflower, chopped
½ cup fresh or frozen green peas
¾lb broccoli, chopped
2 zucchini, chopped

Heat water in pan, stir in spices, simmer until mixture is reduced by half. Add undrained crushed tomatoes, extra water, potatoes, onion, carrots and cauliflower. Bring to boil, simmer, covered, about 10 minutes or until potato is just soft. Add peas, broccoli and zucchini, simmer, covered, further 5 minutes or until liquid is reduced slightly and vegetables are soft.

Serves 2.

■ Not suitable to freeze.
■ Suitable to microwave.
  Total fat: Negligible.

BELOW: From top: Spicy Bean Casserole, Curried Vegetable Hot Pot.
RIGHT: Black-Eyed Bean Soup with Pinwheel Damper.

♥
BLACK-EYED BEAN SOUP WITH PINWHEEL DAMPER

Soup can be made a day ahead. Make damper just before serving.

½ cup black-eyed beans
2 teaspoons olive oil
1 onion, chopped
1 carrot, chopped
5oz sweet potato, chopped
1 small turnip, chopped
1 stalk celery, chopped
1 zucchini, chopped
14½oz can no-added-salt tomatoes
1 cup water
½ vegetable bouillon cube, crumbled
1 teaspoon no-added-salt
   tomato paste

PINWHEEL DAMPER
2 teaspoons olive oil
6 green onions, chopped
¼ cup chopped fresh parsley
1 cup white self-rising flour
½ cup whole-wheat self-rising flour
1 teaspoon sugar
¼ cup skim milk
⅓ cup water, approximately
1 egg white, lightly beaten

Cover beans with water in bowl, stand overnight; drain.

Heat oil in pan, add onion, carrot, sweet potato, turnip and celery, cook 5 minutes. Add beans, zucchini, undrained crushed tomatoes, water, bouillon cube and paste. Bring to boil, simmer, covered, about 45 minutes or until beans are tender. Serve with pinwheel damper.

Pinwheel Damper: Heat oil in pan, add onions and parsley, cook 1 minute; cool.

Sift flours and sugar into bowl, stir in milk and enough water to make a sticky dough. Turn dough onto floured surface, knead gently until smooth.

Roll dough to 8 inch x 12 inch rectangle, spread evenly with onion mixture, roll up dough from long side. Cut roll into 6 slices.

Place slices cut-side-up in greased shallow 7 inch round baking pan, brush tops with egg white. Bake in 400°F oven about 15 minutes or until well browned.

Serves 2.

■ Not suitable to freeze.
■ Not suitable to microwave.
   Total fat: 22.4 grams.
■ Fat per serve: 11.2 grams.

Beef & Veal

♥ ♥ ♥
VEAL CHOPS WITH TANGY LEMON SAUCE

Make recipe close to serving time.

2 x 5oz veal chops

TANGY LEMON SAUCE
1 teaspoon olive oil
1 onion, sliced
3 tablespoons dry white wine
**½ small chicken bouillon
    cube, crumbled**
1 cup water
1 teaspoon granulated sugar
1 teaspoon cornstarch
4 teaspoons water, extra
4 teaspoons fresh lemon juice
4 teaspoons chopped fresh parsley
1 teaspoon chopped fresh thyme

Remove all visible fat from chops. Broil chops until tender; serve with sauce.
Tangy Lemon Sauce: Heat oil in pan, add onion, cook until soft. Stir in wine, bouillon cube, water and sugar, bring to boil, simmer, uncovered, until reduced by one-third. Stir in blended cornstarch and extra water, juice and herbs; stir gently until sauce boils and thickens.

Serves 2.

■ Not suitable to freeze.
■ Not suitable to microwave.
◻ Total fat: 9 grams.
■ Fat per serve: 4.5 grams.

♥ ♥
BEEF AND BEER CASSEROLE

Make casserole close to serving time.

14oz beef top round steak
2 tablespoons all-purpose flour
2 teaspoons olive oil
1 leek, chopped
1 small red bell pepper, chopped
3½oz mushrooms, chopped
1 tomato, peeled, chopped
1 cup beer
½ cup water
**2 teaspoons no-added-salt
    tomato paste**
4 teaspoons chopped fresh parsley
2 teaspoons chopped fresh oregano

Trim all visible fat from steak; slice steak into 4 pieces. Toss steak in flour. Heat oil in pan, add steak, cook until browned on both sides. Remove steak from pan; keep warm.

Add leek, pepper and mushrooms to pan, cook, covered, about 10 minutes or until leek is soft. Add steak, tomato, beer, water and paste, bring to boil. Pour steak mixture into ovenproof dish, cover, bake in 350˚F oven about 1¼ hours or until steak is tender. Stir in herbs just before serving.

Serves 2.

■ Not suitable to freeze.
■ Not suitable to microwave.
◻ Total fat: 18.6 grams.
■ Fat per serve: 9.3 grams.

RIGHT: Clockwise from back: Veal with Marsala Sauce (recipe over page), Veal Chops with Tangy Lemon Sauce, Beef and Beer Casserole.

♥ ♥ ♥
VEAL WITH MARSALA SAUCE

Recipe can be prepared a day ahead.

4 x 2¹⁄₂oz veal steaks
¼ cup marsala
4 teaspoons fresh lemon juice
½ teaspoon olive oil
2 teaspoons cornstarch
¾ cup water
**½ small chicken bouillon
    cube, crumbled**
1 tablespoon plum preserves
1 clove garlic, crushed
3 green onions, chopped

Remove all visible fat from veal. Pound veal thinly. Combine veal with marsala and juice in bowl, refrigerate several hours or overnight.

Drain veal, reserve ¹⁄₃ cup marinade. Heat oil in nonstick skillet, add veal, cook until tender; remove from pan.

Blend cornstarch with reserved marinade in pan, add water, bouillon cube and preserves. Stir over heat until mixture boils and thickens. Stir in garlic and onions. Serve veal with sauce.

Serves 2.

■ Not suitable to freeze.
■ Not suitable to microwave.
   Total fat: 7.7 grams.
■ Fat per serve: 3.9 grams.

♥ ♥ ♥
BEEF AND ONION KABOBS

Recipe is best prepared a day ahead.

¾lb beef top round steak
12 pearl onions

MARINADE
¼ cup honey
¼ cup fresh lemon juice
2 teaspoons grated fresh gingerroot
2 teaspoons Worcestershire sauce
¼ cup no-added-salt tomato ketchup
4 teaspoons chopped fresh oregano

Remove all visible fat from steak, chop steak into bite-sized pieces. Thread steak and onions onto 6 skewers. Place kabobs in shallow dish, add marinade, refrigerate several hours or overnight.

Broil kabobs, brushing with marinade, until steak is tender.
Marinade: Combine all ingredients in bowl; mix well.

Serves 2.

■ Not suitable to freeze.
■ Not suitable to microwave.
   Total fat: 9.6 grams.
■ Fat per serve: 4.8 grams.

RIGHT: Clockwise from back: Sherried Roasted Veal, Beef and Onion Kabobs, Veal Stir-Fry with Bell Peppers and Pecans.

♥ ♥
VEAL STIR-FRY WITH BELL PEPPERS AND PECANS

Make recipe close to serving time.

10oz veal steaks, sliced
1 onion, sliced
1 red bell pepper, sliced
1 green bell pepper, sliced
4 teaspoons chopped fresh
    lemon grass
3 tablespoons pecans, halved
1 teaspoon grated lemon zest
3 tablespoons fresh lemon juice
½ small chicken bouillon
    cube, crumbled
3 tablespoons reduced sodium
    soy sauce
1 clove garlic, minced

Remove all visible fat from veal. Heat wok or nonstick pan, add veal, stir-fry until browned all over. Remove veal from pan; keep warm. Add onion, peppers and lemon grass to wok, stir-fry until vegetables are soft. Stir in nuts, stir-fry 1 minute. Stir in veal with combined zest, juice, bouillon cube, sauce and garlic, stir-fry until heated through.

Serves 2.

- Not suitable to freeze.
- Not suitable to microwave.
- Total fat: 19.4 grams.
- Fat per serve: 9.7 grams.

♥ ♥ ♥
SHERRIED ROASTED VEAL

Recipe is best prepared a day ahead.

1½lb veal boneless loin roast

MARINADE
¼ cup reduced sodium soy sauce
2 teaspoons chopped fresh
    gingerroot
2 green onions, sliced
¼ cup dry sherry
¼ cup honey
4 teaspoons fresh orange juice
½ x 8oz canned sliced water
    chestnuts, drained

Remove all visible fat from veal. Cover veal with marinade in bowl, cover, refrigerate overnight.

Drain veal; reserve marinade. Place veal on rack in roasting pan. Cook, covered, in 400°F oven 15 minutes, reduce heat to 350°F, cook, covered, further 30 minutes or until tender. Heat reserved marinade in pan until boiling, serve with veal.

Marinade: Combine all ingredients in bowl; mix well.

Serves 4.

- Suitable to freeze.
- Not suitable to microwave.
- Total fat: 11.3 grams.
- Fat per serve: 2.8 grams.

♥ ♥
CHILI MEATLOAF WITH
TOMATO SAUCE

Recipe can be made 3 hours ahead.

½lb beef top round steak
¼ cup fresh bread crumbs
1 small onion, chopped
1 clove garlic, minced
¼ teaspoon ground oregano leaves
¼ teaspoon ground cumin
¼ teaspoon ground coriander
¼ teaspoon chili powder
2 egg whites

TOMATO SAUCE
1 teaspoon olive oil
1 small onion, chopped
1 small clove garlic, minced
½ x 14½oz can no-added-salt
  tomatoes
½ teaspoon dark brown sugar
¼ teaspoon chili powder
1 teaspoon Worcestershire sauce

Trim all visible fat from steak. Process all ingredients until smooth, spoon mixture evenly into 2 lightly greased small loaf pans (⅔ cup capacity). Bake in 350°F oven about 45 minutes or until firm and cooked through. Serve with sauce.
Tomato Sauce: Heat oil in pan, add onion, and garlic, cook until soft. Stir in undrained crushed tomatoes and remaining ingredients. Bring to boil, simmer, uncovered, until thick. Blend or process sauce until smooth.

Serves 2.

■ Meatloaf suitable to freeze.
■ Not suitable to microwave.
  Total fat: 12.5 grams.
■ Fat per serve: 6.3 grams.

♥ ♥ ♥
BAKED CRUMBED VEAL

Recipe can be prepared a day ahead.

4 x 2oz veal steaks
3 tablespoons reduced fat
  mayonnaise
½ cup seasoned stuffing mix

Remove all visible fat from steaks. Lightly spread each steak with mayonnaise, coat completely with stuffing mix. Place veal on baking sheet, bake in 400°F oven about 15 minutes or until veal is tender.

Serves 2.

■ Not suitable to freeze.
■ Not suitable to microwave.
  Total fat: 9.5 grams.
■ Fat per serve: 4.8 grams.

♥ ♥
MEATBALLS IN VEGETABLE
PAPRIKA SAUCE

Recipe can be made a day ahead.

½lb beef top round steak
½ cup fresh bread crumbs
4 teaspoons chopped fresh parsley
4 teaspoons chopped fresh chives
1 egg white
1 teaspoon Worcestershire sauce
1 teaspoon olive oil
4 teaspoons chopped fresh basil

SAUCE
14½oz can no-added-salt tomatoes
1 cup water
3 tablespoons dry red wine
1 onion, chopped
1 carrot, chopped
1 stalk celery, chopped
½ teaspoon Worcestershire sauce
½ teaspoon sugar
1 teaspoon paprika

Trim all visible fat from steak, blend or process steak until ground. Combine steak, bread crumbs, parsley, chives, egg white and sauce in bowl. Shape mixture into small meatballs.

Heat oil in nonstick skillet, add meatballs, cook until well browned all over and cooked through, drain on absorbent paper. Add meatballs and basil to sauce, mix well, stir until heated through.
Sauce: Combine undrained crushed tomatoes with remaining ingredients in pan, bring to boil, simmer, uncovered, about 20 minutes or until vegetables are soft. Blend or process sauce until smooth, return mixture to pan to reheat.

Serves 2.

■ Suitable to freeze.
■ Not suitable to microwave.
  Total fat: 13.8 grams.
■ Fat per serve: 6.9 grams.

LEFT: Clockwise from left: Baked Crumbed Veal, Meatballs in Vegetable Paprika Sauce, Chili Meatloaf with Tomato Sauce.

♥♥ VEAL CHOPS WITH TOMATO CILANTRO SAUCE

Make recipe close to serving time.

2 x 5oz veal chops
2 teaspoons olive oil
2 green onions, chopped
1 teaspoon ground cumin
**1 small fresh red chili
   pepper, chopped**
1 clove garlic, minced
1 teaspoon grated fresh gingerroot
4 tomatoes, peeled, chopped
½ cup water
**4 teaspoons no-added-salt
   tomato paste**
4 teaspoons fresh lime juice
2 teaspoon sugar
4 teaspoons chopped fresh cilantro
2 teaspoons chopped fresh mint

Remove all visible fat from veal. Heat oil in pan, add veal, cook until lightly browned on both sides. Remove veal from pan; keep warm.

Add onions, cumin, chili, garlic and gingerroot to pan, cook, stirring, about 2 minutes or until onions are soft. Add veal, tomatoes, water, paste, juice and sugar, simmer, covered, about 10 minutes or until veal is tender. Stir in herbs.

Serves 2.

■ Not suitable to freeze.
■ Not suitable to microwave.
□ Total fat: 14.4 grams.
■ Fat per serve: 7.2 grams.

♥♥♥ PEPPERED VEAL MEDALLIONS

Make recipe just before serving.

4 x 2½oz veal medallions
**3 tablespoons drained green
   peppercorns, crushed**
¼ cup brandy
½ cup buttermilk

Remove all visible fat from veal. Combine veal, peppercorns and brandy in bowl; refrigerate several hours or overnight.

Drain veal, reserve marinade. Cook veal in heated nonstick skillet until tender. Remove from skillet; keep warm. Combine reserved marinade and buttermilk in same skillet, bring to boil, pour over veal just before serving.

Serves 2.

■ Not suitable to freeze.
■ Not suitable to microwave.
□ Total fat: 8.5 grams.
■ Fat per serve: 4.3 grams.

♥ SEASONED BEEF ROLL

Roll can be prepared 2 days ahead.

¾lb piece beef top round steak
2 teaspoons olive oil
2 teaspoons all-purpose flour
¼ cup dry red wine
¼ cup water
½ small beef bouillon cube, crumbled

SEASONING
½ cup old-fashioned oats
¼ cup water
1 teaspoon olive oil
1 small onion, chopped
1 clove garlic, minced
3 tablespoons dried currants
3 tablespoons chopped fresh chives
¼ teaspoon sugar

Remove all visible fat from steak. Place steak between 2 sheets of plastic. Pound out to a thin rectangle, spread with seasoning, roll up from narrow end like a jelly-roll; secure roll with kitchen string.

Heat oil in nonstick roasting pan, add roll, cook over heat until browned all over. Bake, uncovered, in 350°F oven about 20 minutes or until tender. Remove roll from dish, cover while preparing sauce.

Add flour to dish, stir over heat about 1 minute or until well browned. Remove from heat, gradually stir in combined wine, water and bouillon cube. Stir over heat until sauce boils and thickens; strain. Remove string from roll, slice roll and serve with sauce.

Seasoning: Combine oats and water in bowl, stand 10 minutes. Heat oil in pan, add onion and garlic, cook until soft. Combine onion mixture, oat mixture, currants, chives and sugar in bowl.

Serves 2.

■ Suitable to freeze.
■ Not suitable to microwave.
□ Total fat: 26.6 grams.
■ Fat per serve: 13.3 grams.

ABOVE: Seasoned Beef Roll.
RIGHT: Clockwise from back right: Beef in Red Wine (recipe over page), Peppered Veal Medallions, Veal Chops with Tomato Cilantro Sauce.

70

♥ ♥
BEEF IN RED WINE

Recipe can be made a day ahead.

¾lb boneless top blade steak
2 onions, chopped
1 clove garlic, minced
½ small green bell pepper, chopped
1 stalk celery, chopped
2 carrots, chopped
3½oz mushrooms, sliced
15oz can tomato puree
2 teaspoons Worcestershire sauce
½ cup dry red wine
1 teaspoon dried mixed herbs

Trim all visible fat from steak, cut steak evenly into cubes. Combine steak with remaining ingredients in pan, bring to boil, simmer, covered, about 1½ hours, or until steak is tender.

Serves 2.

■ Not suitable to freeze.
■ Not suitable to microwave.
　 Total fat: 15 grams.
■ Fat per serve: 7.5 grams.

♥ ♥ ♥
BEEF AND MUSHROOM CASSEROLE

Recipe can be made a day ahead.

¾lb boneless beef chuck
4 teaspoons all-purpose flour
¼ cup water
3½oz button mushrooms
3½oz pearl onions
½ cup dry red wine
1 cup water, extra
4 teaspoons no-added-salt
　 tomato paste
1 bay leaf

Remove all visible fat from steak, cut steak into bite-sized pieces. Toss steak in flour. Heat water in pan, stir in steak, cook 3 minutes, stir in remaining ingredients. Bring to boil, simmer, covered, about 1½ hours or until steak is tender. Remove bay leaf before serving.

Serves 2.

■ Not suitable to freeze.
■ Not suitable to microwave.
　 Total fat: 8.7 grams.
■ Fat per serve: 4.4 grams.

*ABOVE: Beef and Mushroom Casserole.
RIGHT: Beef and Pear with Garlic Mustard
Sauce.*

♥ ♥
BEEF AND PEAR WITH GARLIC MUSTARD SAUCE

Make recipe close to serving time.

1 pear, halved
¾ cup water
½ cup fresh orange juice
¾lb beef tenderloin steak
½ teaspoon olive oil
2 cloves garlic, minced
2 teaspoons seeded mustard
2 teaspoons cornstarch
4 teaspoons brandy
1 clove garlic, minced, extra

Combine pear, water and juice in pan, bring to boil, cool pear in liquid.

Remove all visible fat from steak. Heat oil in nonstick skillet, add steak, cook until well browned and tender. Remove steak from pan; keep warm.

Drain pear, reserving 1¼ cups liquid. Add garlic and mustard to same skillet, cook 1 minute. Stir in blended cornstarch and reserved liquid, stir over heat until mixture boils and thickens. Stir in brandy and extra garlic. Slice beef, serve with sliced pear and sauce.

Serves 2.

■ Not suitable to freeze.
■ Not suitable to microwave.
　 Total fat: 15.5 grams.
■ Fat per serve: 7.8 grams.

❤ ❤
LAMB LOIN WITH HAZELNUT CHIVE CRUST

Recipe can be prepared 3 hours ahead.

1½lb lamb loin roast
8 spinach leaves
½ cup fresh bread crumbs
¼ cup chopped roasted
　　unsalted hazelnuts
¼ cup chopped fresh chives
3 tablespoons port wine
4 teaspoons chutney

Trim all visible fat from lamb, open lamb flat on bench.

Drop spinach in boiling water for 30 seconds, rinse in cold water, drain well; pat dry with absorbent paper. Place spinach evenly over lamb, roll lamb tightly; secure with skewers.

Combine remaining ingredients in bowl, press firmly over surface of lamb. Place lamb on rack in roasting pan, bake in 350°F oven about 1 hour or until tender.

Serves 4.
- ■ Suitable to freeze.
- ■ Not suitable to microwave.
- ☐ Total fat: 28 grams.
- ■ Fat per serve: 7 grams.

❤ ❤
LAMB FILLETS WITH VEGETABLE SAUCE

Make recipe just before serving.

4 (10oz) lamb fillets
½ cup sweet sherry
1 cup water
1 carrot, chopped
½ red bell pepper, chopped
1 tomato, chopped
1 stalk celery, chopped
1 onion, chopped
4 teaspoons lowfat plain yogurt
4 teaspoons chopped fresh oregano
1 clove garlic, minced

Trim all visible fat from lamb. Cook lamb over heat in roasting pan until lamb is browned all over. Remove lamb from pan.

Add sherry and water to pan, bring to boil, remove from heat. Add carrot, pepper, tomato, celery and onion to pan, bake, covered, in 375°F oven about 20 minutes or until vegetables are soft.

Place lamb on vegetables in pan, bake further 10 minutes or until lamb is tender. Remove lamb from pan; keep warm while making sauce.

Blend or process vegetable mixture until smooth, push through fine sieve, stir in yogurt, oregano and garlic. Serve lamb with sauce.

Serves 2.
- ■ Not suitable to freeze.
- ■ Not suitable to microwave.
- ☐ Total fat: 10.8 grams.
- ■ Fat per serve: 5.4 grams.

❤ ❤ ❤
HONEYED GINGERROOT LAMB KABOBS

Recipe is best prepared a day ahead.

1½lb leg of lamb, boned

MARINADE
¾ cup green ginger wine
4 teaspoons honey
¼ cup mint jelly
2 teaspoons grated fresh gingerroot
2 teaspoons reduced sodium
　　soy sauce

Trim visible fat from lamb, cut into cubes.

Thread lamb onto 6 skewers. Place kabobs in shallow dish, add marinade; refrigerate overnight. Broil kabobs, brushing with marinade, until tender.
Marinade: Combine ingredients in bowl.

Serves 2.
- ■ Not suitable to freeze.
- ■ Not suitable to microwave.
- ☐ Total fat: 6.6 grams.
- ■ Fat per serve: 3.3 grams.

LEFT: Lamb Loin with Hazelnut Chive Crust.
ABOVE: From top: Honeyed Gingerroot Lamb Kabobs, Lamb Fillets with Vegetable Sauce.

♥ ♥
LAMB KIBBE WITH TAHINI SAUCE

Make recipe close to serving time.
Sauce can be made 3 hours ahead.

¼ cup bulgur
½lb lamb leg chops
1 small onion, chopped
1 tablespoon chopped pine nuts
1 egg white
3 tablespoons chopped fresh parsley
4 teaspoons chopped fresh mint
½ teaspoon dried oregano leaves
¼ teaspoon dried basil leaves

TAHINI SAUCE
3 tablespoons lowfat plain yogurt
1 teaspoon tahini (sesame paste)
1 teaspoon reduced sodium soy
    sauce
1 teaspoon chopped fresh parsley

Grease deep 6 inch square baking pan.
Cover bulgur with cold water in bowl,
stand 1 hour, drain well; squeeze out
excess moisture.

Trim all visible fat from lamb, blend or
process lamb until ground. Combine
bulgur, lamb, onion, nuts, egg white,
parsley, mint, oregano and basil in bowl;
press mixture into prepared pan. Bake in
350˚F oven about 40 minutes or until
cooked through. Cut into 4 squares, serve
with tahini sauce.

Tahini Sauce: Combine all ingredients in
bowl; mix well.

Serves 2.

■ Kibbe suitable to freeze.
■ Not suitable to microwave.
□ Total fat: 16.5 grams.
■ Fat per serve: 8.3 grams.

RIGHT: Clockwise from front: Lamb Hot
Pot with Couscous, Lamb and Yogurt
Curry (recipe over page), Lamb Kibbe with
Tahini Sauce.
FAR RIGHT: Lamb Fillets in Herb Marinade.

♥
LAMB HOT POT WITH COUSCOUS

Hot pot can be made several hours ahead. Couscous is best made close to serving time.

1¼lb lamb leg chops
4 teaspoons all-purpose flour
2 teaspoons olive oil
1 onion, sliced
1 teaspoon ground cinnamon
1 teaspoon turmeric
1½ cups water
½ small beef bouillon cube, crumbled
3½oz prunes, pitted

COUSCOUS
2 cups boiling water
1 cup couscous

Trim all visible fat from lamb, cut lamb into cubes; toss in flour.

Heat oil in pan, add onion, cook until soft. Add lamb, cook until lamb is browned all over. Stir in cinnamon and turmeric, cook 1 minute. Stir in water, bouillon cube and prunes, bring to boil, simmer, covered, about 30 minutes or until lamb is tender. Serve lamb with couscous.

Couscous: Pour water over couscous, stand 8 minutes, stir with a fork.

Serves 2.

■ Not suitable to freeze.
■ Not suitable to microwave.
  Total fat: 28.8 grams.
■ Fat per serve: 14.4 grams.

♥ ♥
LAMB FILLETS IN HERB MARINADE

Recipe best prepared 3 hours ahead.

10½oz lamb fillets
2 teaspoons cracked black peppercorns

HERB MARINADE
2 teaspoons olive oil
1½ tablespoons tarragon vinegar
4 teaspoons water
2 teaspoons sugar
1 teaspoon drained green peppercorns
¼ teaspoon dry mustard
2 green onions, chopped
2 teaspoons chopped fresh parsley
1 teaspoon chopped fresh thyme

Trim all visible fat from fillets. Press peppercorns onto fillets. Place fillets onto greased baking sheet, bake in 375˚F oven about 25 minutes or until tender, drain on absorbent paper; cool.

Slice lamb, place in bowl, cover with marinade, refrigerate several hours before serving.

Herb Marinade: Combine all ingredients in bowl; mix well.

Serves 2.

■ Not suitable to freeze.
■ Not suitable to microwave.
  Total fat: 19.8 grams.
■ Fat per serve: 9.9 grams.

Spoon mixture evenly into shallow ovenproof dish (3 cup capacity).

Spoon topping mixture into large piping bag fitted with a fluted tube; pipe onto pie. Bake in 350°F oven about 40 minutes or until topping is lightly browned.

Topping: Boil, steam or microwave potatoes until soft. Mash potatoes in bowl until free of lumps. Beat potatoes and milk with electric mixer until light and fluffy.

Serves 2.

- ■ Not suitable to freeze.
- ■ Not suitable to microwave.
- □ Total fat: 24 grams.
- ■ Fat per serve: 12 grams.

♥ ♥

CRUMBED LAMB WITH ONION MARMALADE

Marmalade can be made 3 days ahead. Cook lamb just before serving.

4 x 2½oz lamb fillets
½ cup fresh bread crumbs
4 teaspoons chopped fresh parsley
¼ teaspoon paprika
½ teaspoon olive oil

ONION MARMALADE
2 onions, sliced
¾ cup water
1 teaspoon grated orange zest
¼ cup fresh orange juice
¼ cup brown vinegar
⅓ cup dark brown sugar

Trim fat from lamb. Roll lamb in combined bread crumbs, parsley and paprika; press crumbs on firmly.

Brush small baking sheet with the oil, place lamb on baking sheet, bake in 375°F oven about 10 minutes or until cooked as desired. Serve lamb with onion marmalade.

Onion Marmalade: Combine onions and water in pan, cook, covered, about 15 minutes or until very soft. Add zest, juice, vinegar and sugar, stir over heat until sugar is dissolved. Bring to boil, simmer, uncovered, about 30 minutes or until marmalade is thick.

Serves 2.

- ■ Not suitable to freeze.
- ■ Not suitable to microwave.
- □ Total fat: 13 grams.
- ■ Fat per serve: 6.5 grams.

♥ ♥ ♥

LAMB AND YOGURT CURRY

Recipe can be made a day ahead.

1½lb leg of lamb, boned
1 large onion, chopped
1 teaspoon grated fresh gingerroot
1 clove garlic, minced
1 teaspoon chili powder
1 teaspoon ground coriander
2 teaspoons ground cumin
½ teaspoon ground black pepper
1 teaspoon garam masala
1 teaspoon dry mustard
1 teaspoon turmeric
¼ teaspoon ground cardamom
3 tablespoons fresh lemon juice
1 cup water
½ cup lowfat plain yogurt

Trim fat from lamb; cut lamb into cubes. Combine lamb cubes and remaining ingredients, except yogurt, in pan. Simmer, covered, about 1½ hours, or until lamb is tender and liquid is reduced by half; remove from heat, stir in yogurt.

Serves 2.

- ■ Suitable to freeze.
- ■ Suitable to microwave.
- □ Total fat: 6.6 grams.
- ■ Fat per serve: 3.3 grams.

♥

SHEPHERD'S PIE

Pie can be made 2 days ahead.

1½lb lamb sirloin chops
1 teaspoon olive oil
1 onion, chopped
1 carrot, chopped
¾ cup water
4 teaspoons no-added-salt tomato paste
1 teaspoon reduced sodium soy sauce
1 teaspoon Worcestershire sauce
½ small chicken bouillon cube, crumbled
4 teaspoons all-purpose flour
3 tablespoons water, extra

TOPPING
2 large (1lb) potatoes, chopped
¼ cup skim milk

Remove lamb from bones, trim all visible fat from lamb. (You should have about 10oz lean lamb.) Blend or process lamb until ground.

Heat oil in pan, stir in lamb, onion and carrot, stir until lamb is browned all over. Stir in water, paste, sauces and bouillon cube, bring to boil, simmer, uncovered, 5 minutes. Stir in blended flour and extra water, stir until mixture boils and thickens.

ABOVE: Shepherd's Pie.
RIGHT: Crumbed Lamb with Onion Marmalade.

Pork

♥
OATY PORK WITH APPLE AND PEPPERCORN SAUCE

Pork can be prepared several hours ahead. Sauce is best made close to serving time.

2 x 7oz pork loin medallions
4 teaspoons all-purpose flour
1 egg white, lightly beaten
½ cup old-fashioned oats
1 tablespoon olive oil

APPLE AND PEPPERCORN SAUCE
⅔ cup water
4 teaspoons dry white wine
½ small chicken bouillon
** cube, crumbled**
1 apple, sliced
2 teaspoons cornstarch
4 teaspoons water, extra
1 teaspoon drained green
** peppercorns, crushed**

Trim all visible fat from pork. Toss pork in flour, dip in egg white, then oats. Press oats firmly onto pork; cover, refrigerate 30 minutes.

Heat oil in pan, add pork, cook until browned and tender. Serve with sauce.

Apple and Peppercorn Sauce: Combine water, wine and bouillon cube in pan, bring to boil, add apple, simmer, covered, until apple is tender. Remove apple from pan, drain on absorbent paper. Stir blended cornstarch and extra water into pan, stir until mixture boils and thickens. Stir in peppercorns and apple.

Serves 2.

■ Not suitable to freeze.
■ Not suitable to microwave.
□ Total fat: 23.6 grams.
■ Fat per serve: 11.8 grams.

RIGHT: Clockwise from front: Rosemary Pork with Mandarin Sauce, Apricot and Mint Pork Medallions, Oaty Pork with Apple and Peppercorn Sauce.

♥ ♥
ROSEMARY PORK WITH MANDARIN SAUCE

You will need 2 mandarins for this recipe. Recipe is best made close to serving time.

10oz pork tenderloin
2 teaspoons olive oil
½ cup water
4 teaspoons Grand Marnier
½ small chicken bouillon cube, crumbled

MANDARIN SAUCE
2 teaspoons cornstarch
4 teaspoons water, extra
½ cup fresh mandarin juice
2 teaspoons chopped fresh rosemary

Trim all visible fat from pork. Heat oil in skillet, add pork, cook until browned all over. Place pork on rack in roasting pan.

Add water, liqueur and bouillon cube to skillet, bring to boil, pour into roasting pan. Bake, covered, in 350˚F oven about 20 minutes or until pork is just cooked through. Remove pork and rack. Serve with sauce.

Mandarin Sauce: Stir combined blended cornstarch and extra water with juice into roasting pan, stir over heat until mixture boils and thickens, stir in rosemary.

Serves 2.

- Not suitable to freeze.
- Not suitable to microwave.
  Total fat: 14.1 grams.
- Fat per serve: 7 grams.

♥ ♥ ♥
APRICOT AND MINT PORK MEDALLIONS

Recipe best made just before serving.

4 x 3oz pork loin medallions
16oz can apricot halves, drained
4 teaspoons chopped fresh mint

Trim all visible fat from pork. Cut a pocket along 1 side of each medallion.

Chop half the apricots, blend or process remaining apricots until smooth; reserve apricot puree. Fill pockets with combined chopped apricots and mint; secure openings with toothpicks.

Cook pork in heated nonstick skillet, brushing with reserved apricot puree, until well browned and just cooked through. Serve pork immediately with remaining heated apricot puree.

Serves 2.

- Not suitable to freeze.
- Not suitable to microwave.
  Total fat: 7 grams.
- Fat per serve: 3.5 grams.

♥ ♥ ♥
PORK WITH CHERRY SAUCE

Sauce can be made a day ahead. Pork is best cooked just before serving.

2 x 7oz pork butterfly chops
1 teaspoon olive oil

CHERRY SAUCE
½ x 16½oz can pitted black cherries
4 teaspoons cornstarch
2 teaspoons water
1 teaspoon port wine
½ teaspoon grated lemon zest

Trim all visible fat from pork. Heat oil in nonstick skillet, add pork, cook until well browned and just cooked through. Serve pork with cherry sauce.

Cherry Sauce: Drain cherries, reserve syrup. Combine reserved syrup and blended cornstarch and water in pan, stir over heat until mixture boils and thickens. Stir in cherries, port wine and zest, stir until heated through.

Serves 2.

- ■ Not suitable to freeze.
- ■ Not suitable to microwave.
- ☐ Total fat: 6.5 grams.
- ■ Fat per serve: 3.3 grams.

RIGHT: Clockwise from back left: Pork in Pastry with Cucumber Salad, Pork and Apple Kabobs (recipe over page), Chili Pork and Bean Feast.
BELOW: Pork with Cherry Sauce.

♥ ♥ ♥
PORK IN PASTRY WITH CUCUMBER SALAD

Pork is best prepared close to serving time. Cucumber salad can be made a day ahead.

10oz pork tenderloin
4 teaspoons mint jelly
4 sheets phyllo pastry

CUCUMBER SALAD
3 small green cucumbers, sliced
4 teaspoons cider vinegar
4 teaspoons chopped fresh mint
4 teaspoons mint jelly
2 teaspoons reduced sodium soy sauce
4 teaspoons dry sherry

Trim all visible fat from pork. Cut pork lengthways into 4 strips, combine with jelly, refrigerate 2 hours.

Fold a sheet of pastry in half. Place 1 piece of pork diagonally across pastry, roll up firmly, twist ends to seal. Repeat with remaining pork and pastry. Place pork on baking sheet, bake in 375°F oven about 15 minutes or until pastry is well browned and pork is just cooked through. Serve with cucumber salad.

Cucumber Salad: Combine cucumbers, vinegar, mint, jelly, sauce and sherry in bowl; refrigerate 2 hours.

Serves 2.

- ■ Not suitable to freeze.
- ■ Not suitable to microwave.
- ☐ Total fat: 5 grams.
- ■ Fat per serve 2.5 grams.

♥ ♥ ♥
CHILI PORK AND BEAN FEAST

Recipe can be made 2 days ahead.

1¼lb pork butterfly chops
1 teaspoon olive oil
1 clove garlic, minced
1 onion, chopped
1 cup water
14½oz can no-added-salt tomatoes
1 green bell pepper, chopped
4 teaspoons no-added-salt tomato paste
½ teaspoon chili powder
½ teaspoon ground cumin
½ teaspoon ground coriander
8¾oz can red kidney beans, rinsed, drained

Trim all visible fat from pork (you should have 10oz trimmed pork). Blend or process pork until ground.

Heat oil in pan, add garlic and onion, cook until soft. Stir in pork, stir until browned all over. Stir in water, undrained crushed tomatoes, pepper, paste, chili, cumin and coriander. Bring to boil, simmer, uncovered, 30 minutes. Stir in beans, stir until heated through.

Serves 2.

- ■ Not suitable to freeze.
- ■ Not suitable to microwave.
- ☐ Total fat: 7.5 grams.
- ■ Fat per serve: 3.8 grams.

♥ ♥ ♥
PORK AND APPLE KABOBS

Recipe is best prepared a day ahead.

10oz pork tenderloin
½ cup honey
¼ cup reduced sodium soy sauce
1 teaspoon chili sauce
1 clove garlic, minced
1 teaspoon grated fresh gingerroot
3 tablespoons fresh lemon juice
2 apples, chopped

Trim all visible fat from pork, cut pork into cubes. Combine pork, honey, sauces, garlic, gingerroot and juice in bowl; refrigerate several hours or overnight.

Thread pork and apples alternately onto skewers. Broil kabobs, brushing with marinade, until just cooked through.

Serves 2.

■ Not suitable to freeze.
■ Not suitable to microwave.
□ Total fat: 5 grams.
■ Fat per serve: 2.5 grams.

♥ ♥
PORK WITH PORT AND MUSHROOM SAUCE

Make recipe close to serving time.

2 x 5oz pork butterfly chops

PORT AND MUSHROOM SAUCE
1 small onion, chopped
½ stalk celery, chopped
½ small chicken bouillon
    cube, crumbled
1 cup water
2 teaspoons olive oil
2 teaspoons all-purpose flour
¼ cup water, extra
1 teaspoon Worcestershire sauce
3 tablespoons port wine
3½oz small button mushrooms

Trim all visible fat from pork. Broil pork until well browned and just cooked through. Serve pork with port and mushroom sauce.

Port and Mushroom Sauce: Combine onion, celery, bouillon cube and water in pan, bring to boil, simmer, uncovered, about 5 minutes or until liquid is reduced by half, strain; reserve liquid.

Heat oil in pan, add flour, cook until bubbling. Remove from heat, gradually stir in reserved liquid, extra water, sauce, port wine and mushrooms, stir over heat until sauce boils and thickens.

Serves 2.

■ Not suitable to freeze.
■ Not suitable to microwave.
□ Total fat: 11 grams.
■ Fat per serve: 5.5 grams.

♥ ♥ ♥
STIR-FRIED PORK WITH BLACK BEANS

Make recipe just before serving.

7oz pork tenderloin, thinly sliced
1 egg white, lightly beaten
4 teaspoons dry sherry
3 tablespoons reduced sodium
    soy sauce
13oz broccoli
1 bunch bok choy
½ cup cold water
1 leek, chopped
½lb green beans, chopped
½lb fresh asparagus, chopped
4 teaspoons canned black beans,
    rinsed, drained
½ cup boiling water
3 tablespoons honey
4 teaspoons brown vinegar
4 teaspoons reduced sodium soy
    sauce, extra
1 teaspoon grated fresh gingerroot
2 teaspoons cornstarch

Trim all visible fat from pork. Combine pork, egg white, sherry and sauce in bowl; refrigerate overnight.

Cook pork in heated nonstick skillet until well browned and just cooked through; remove from skillet.

Slice broccoli and bok choy stems lengthways into thin strips. Chop broccoli heads, shred bok choy leaves. Boil, steam or microwave broccoli and bok choy stems until just soft, drain.

Heat cold water in wok or skillet, add leek, cook until soft. Add green beans, asparagus and broccoli, stir until beans are just tender. Mash black beans in bowl with boiling water until smooth, stir in honey, vinegar, extra sauce, gingerroot and cornstarch.

Add pork with black bean mixture to wok, stir-fry over heat until mixture boils and thickens, toss through bok choy leaves. Serve pork mixture over broccoli and bok choy stems.

Serves 2.

■ Not suitable to freeze.
■ Not suitable to microwave.
□ Total fat: 3.4 grams.
■ Fat per serve: 1.7 grams.

RIGHT: From top: Stir-Fried Pork with Black Beans, Pork with Port and Mushroom Sauce.

Vegetables

& Salads

♥ ♥ ♥
BROCCOLI AND APPLE SALAD

Make recipe close to serving time.

10oz broccoli, chopped
2 apples, chopped
½ cup cider vinegar
4 teaspoons fresh lemon juice
¾ cup apple juice
2 tablespoons honey

Boil, steam or microwave broccoli until just tender, rinse in cold water; drain. Combine broccoli and apples in bowl, stir in combined vinegar, juices and honey; refrigerate before serving.

Serves 2.

■ Not suitable to freeze.
■ Suitable to microwave.
  Total fat: Negligible.

♥ ♥ ♥
HOT POTATO SALAD WITH APRICOTS

Recipe can be made a day ahead.

½lb baby potatoes, sliced
5oz green beans, sliced
1 onion, sliced
7oz cherry tomatoes
¼ cup dried apricots, sliced

DRESSING
1 teaspoon cornstarch
½ cup skim milk
3 tablespoons chopped fresh mint
3 tablespoons lowfat plain yogurt

Boil, steam or microwave potatoes and beans separately until tender; drain. Combine potatoes, beans, onion, tomatoes and apricots in bowl. Pour dressing over.
Dressing: Blend cornstarch with milk in pan, stir over heat until mixture boils and thickens. Remove from heat, stir in mint; cool slightly. Stir in yogurt.

Serves 2.

■ Not suitable to freeze.
■ Suitable to microwave.
  Total fat: Negligible.

LEFT: Clockwise from back: Broccoli and Apple Salad, Bell Pepper and Pasta Salad (recipe over page), Hot Potato Salad with Apricots.

♥ ♥ ♥
BELL PEPPER AND PASTA SALAD

Recipe can be made a day ahead.

2 red bell peppers, halved
1 green bell pepper, halved
1 cup (3½oz) penne pasta
4 green onions, chopped

DRESSING
4 teaspoons fresh lemon juice
4 teaspoons red wine vinegar
4 teaspoons honey
1 teaspoon chopped fresh dill

Remove seeds from peppers, place peppers on baking sheet, skin-side-up. Broil until skins are blistered and blackened; peel away skins, slice peppers thinly.

Add pasta to large pan of boiling water, boil, uncovered, until just tender; drain. Combine peppers, pasta and onions in bowl, add dressing.

Dressing: Combine all ingredients in bowl; mix well.

Serves 2.

■ Not suitable to freeze.
■ Not suitable to microwave.
  Total fat: 1 gram.
■ Fat per serve: Negligible.

♥ ♥ ♥
HERBED RICE MOLD

Recipe can be made 3 hours ahead.

1 cup (7oz) brown rice
6 cherry tomatoes, halved
¼ cup chopped fresh parsley
¼ cup chopped fresh chives
4 teaspoons chopped fresh thyme
1 teaspoon olive oil
3 tablespoons fresh lemon juice

Grease a mold (3 cup capacity). Add rice to pan of boiling water, boil, uncovered, about 35 minutes or until rice is tender, drain; cool.

Arrange tomatoes over base of prepared mold. Combine rice, parsley, chives, thyme, oil and juice in bowl. Spoon rice mixture over tomatoes. Press rice mixture firmly into mold. Turn onto plate before serving.

Serves 2.

■ Not suitable to freeze.
■ Not suitable to microwave.
  Total fat: 8.5 grams.
■ Fat per serve: 4.3 grams.

RIGHT: From top: Herbed Rice Mold, Confetti Coleslaw, Green Peas with Leek and Mushrooms.
FAR RIGHT: Lima Beans with Okra.

♥ ♥ ♥
CONFETTI COLESLAW

Make recipe close to serving time.

1 cup (2½oz) shredded cabbage
1 cup (2½oz) shredded red cabbage
1 small carrot, grated
2 green onions, chopped
4 teaspoons reduced fat mayonnaise
4 teaspoons water

Combine all ingredients in bowl.
Serves 2.

■ Not suitable to freeze.
　 Total fat: 2.6 grams.
■ Fat per serve: 1.3 grams.

♥ ♥ ♥
GREEN PEAS WITH LEEK AND MUSHROOMS

Make recipe close to serving time.

5oz green peas
½ leek, sliced
½ vegetable bouillon cube, crumbled
¾ cup water
3½oz button mushrooms
4 teaspoons chopped fresh mint

Combine peas, leek, bouillon cube and water in pan, bring to boil, simmer, covered, until peas are tender. Stir in mushrooms, simmer, covered, until mushrooms are just tender. Stir in mint just before serving.
Serves 2.

■ Not suitable to freeze.
■ Suitable to microwave.
　 Total fat: Negligible.

♥ ♥ ♥
LIMA BEANS WITH OKRA

Recipe can be made a day ahead.

1 cup (7oz) dried lima beans
1 onion, chopped
1 clove garlic, minced
14½oz can no-added-salt tomatoes
1 cup water
½ small chicken bouillon
**　 cube, crumbled**
1lb okra
3 tablespoons brown vinegar
1 tomato, chopped
3 tablespoons chopped fresh parsley
1 clove garlic, minced, extra

Place beans in bowl, cover with hot water, stand several hours or overnight; drain.
　Combine beans, onion, garlic, undrained crushed tomatoes, water and bouillon cube in pan, simmer, covered, 40 minutes or until beans are tender.
　Top and tail okra, rinse well; drain. Stir okra and vinegar into pan, simmer, covered, further 10 minutes. Stir in tomato, parsley and extra garlic, stir until heated through.
Serves 2.

■ Not suitable to freeze.
■ Not suitable to microwave.
　 Total fat: 3.2 grams.
■ Fat per serve: 1.6 grams.

♥ ♥ ♥
ZUCCHINI POTATO FRITTATA

Make recipe just before serving.

2 large (1lb) potatoes
1 zucchini
3 tablespoons chopped fresh parsley
1 teaspoon olive oil

Coarsely grate potatoes and zucchini; drain well on absorbent paper. Combine potatoes, zucchini and parsley in bowl.

Heat half the oil in nonstick omelet pan. Using an egg slice, press potato mixture evenly over base of pan, cook, uncovered, about 10 minutes or until lightly browned underneath. Turn frittata carefully onto a plate.

Heat remaining oil in same pan, carefully slide frittata, browned-side-up into pan. Cook further 10 minutes or until lightly browned underneath. Transfer frittata to plate, cut into wedges.

Serves 2.

■ Not suitable to freeze.
■ Not suitable to microwave.
□ Total fat: 4.5 grams.
■ Fat per serve: 2.3 grams.

♥ ♥ ♥
MIXED VEGETABLES WITH TARRAGON VINAIGRETTE

Make recipe just before serving.

1 small golden nugget squash,
  chopped
6 baby potatoes, halved
3½oz snow peas

TARRAGON VINAIGRETTE
2 teaspoons chopped fresh tarragon
2 tablespoons white wine vinegar
2 teaspoons olive oil
½ teaspoon cracked black pepper
¼ teaspoon sugar

Boil, steam or microwave squash, potatoes and snow peas separately until just tender; drain. Combine vegetables in bowl, add vinaigrette.
Tarragon Vinaigrette: Combine all ingredients in jar; shake well.

Serves 2.

■ Not suitable to freeze.
■ Suitable to microwave.
□ Total fat: 9 grams.
■ Fat per serve: 4.5 grams.

RIGHT: Clockwise from back: Zucchini and Potato Frittata, Zucchini Mushroom Salad (recipe over page), Mixed Vegetables with Tarragon Vinaigrette.

♥ ♥ ♥
ZUCCHINI MUSHROOM SALAD

Make recipe close to serving time.

7oz zucchini, sliced
5oz button mushrooms, sliced

DRESSING
2 teaspoons chopped fresh mint
4 teaspoons fresh lemon juice
1 teaspoon seeded mustard
3 tablespoons reduced fat
    coleslaw dressing

Combine zucchini, mushrooms and dressing in bowl, toss gently.
Dressing: Combine all ingredients in jar; shake well.

Serves 2.

■ Not suitable to freeze.
    Total fat: 1.8 grams.
■ Fat per serve: Negligible.

♥ ♥ ♥
COUSCOUS AND MINT SALAD

Salad can be made 3 hours ahead.

½ cup couscous
½ cup boiling water
½ small chicken bouillon
    cube, crumbled
1 small green cucumber, chopped
1 tomato, chopped
1 carrot, grated
½ small red bell pepper, chopped
¼ cup chopped fresh mint
3 tablespoons fresh lemon juice
1 teaspoon olive oil

Combine couscous, water and bouillon cube in small bowl, stand 10 minutes or until all water has been absorbed. Stir in cucumber, tomato, carrot, pepper and mint. Stir in combined juice and oil just before serving.

Serves 2.

■ Not suitable to freeze.
    Total fat: 4.5 grams.
■ Fat per serve: 2.3 grams.

♥ ♥ ♥
BEANS WITH MINT GLAZE

Make recipe close to serving time.

1½lb broad beans, shelled
3½oz green beans, sliced
2 carrots, chopped

MINT GLAZE
1 tablespoon dry sherry
½ vegetable bouillon cube, crumbled
2 teaspoons cornstarch
4 teaspoons water
2 teaspoons chopped fresh mint

Place vegetables in pan, with enough water to cover, bring to boil, simmer, uncovered, until just tender, drain; reserve ⅔ cup of the liquid for mint glaze. Serve vegetables with glaze.
Mint Glaze: Combine reserved liquid, sherry, bouillon cube and blended cornstarch and water in pan. Stir over heat until mixture boils and thickens, remove from heat; stir in mint.

Serves 2.

■ Not suitable to freeze.
■ Not suitable to microwave.
    Total fat: Negligible.

BELOW: Couscous and Mint Salad.
RIGHT: Beans with Mint Glaze.

♥ ♥ ♥
CAULIFLOWER TIMBALES WITH MUSTARD SAUCE

Make recipe just before serving.

1 small red bell pepper
¼lb cauliflower, chopped
¼ cup buttermilk
2 egg whites, lightly beaten
4 teaspoons nonfat dry milk
1 teaspoon arrowroot
½ teaspoon sugar

MUSTARD SAUCE
1 green onion, chopped
4 teaspoons dry white wine
1 teaspoon honey
2 teaspoons red wine vinegar
4 teaspoons fresh lemon juice
1 teaspoon seeded mustard

Cut 2 long ½ inch strips from pepper; boil, steam or microwave strips until tender; drain. Thinly slice remaining pepper; reserve for sauce.

Boil, steam or microwave cauliflower until soft; drain. Blend or process cauliflower until smooth, push through sieve (you will need ¼ cup cauliflower puree). Combine buttermilk, egg whites, dry milk, arrowroot and sugar in bowl. Stir in cauliflower puree.

Pour mixture into 2 wetted timbale molds (½ cup capacity), cover each mold with foil. Place molds into roasting pan with enough boiling water to come half way up sides of molds.

Bake in 375°F oven about 35 minutes or until timbales are just set, stand 5 minutes; turn onto plates. Wrap a strip of bell pepper around each timbale, serve with mustard sauce.

Mustard Sauce: Combine reserved bell pepper with remaining ingredients in pan, bring to boil, remove from heat.

Serves 2.

■ Not suitable to freeze.
■ Not suitable to microwave.
   Total fat: 2.5 grams.
■ Fat per serve: 1.3 grams.

♥ ♥ ♥
GOLDEN POTATO STICKS

Make recipe just before serving.

2 large (1lb) potatoes, chopped
4 teaspoons nonfat dry milk
4 teaspoons chopped fresh tarragon
3 tablespoons grated Parmesan cheese

Boil, steam or microwave potatoes until soft, drain; mash well with fork. Stir in dry milk and tarragon. Spoon mixture into large piping bag fitted with a large fluted tube. Pipe 2 inch lengths of mixture onto baking paper-covered baking sheet, sprinkle with cheese. Bake in 400°F oven about 20 minutes or until slightly puffed and browned.

Serves 2.

■ Not suitable to freeze.
■ Not suitable to microwave.
   Total fat: 6.3 grams.
■ Fat per serve: 3.2 grams.

♥ ♥ ♥
BAKED CARROT LOAF

Make recipe just before serving.

3 medium (10oz) carrots, chopped
1 onion, chopped
½ small chicken bouillon cube, crumbled
½ teaspoon ground black pepper
¾ cup water
3 egg whites
¼ cup skim milk

Combine carrots, onion, bouillon cube, pepper and water in pan. Bring to boil, simmer, covered, until vegetables are soft; drain. Blend or process mixture until smooth, push through fine sieve; cool. Stir in egg whites and milk.

Pour mixture into 3 inch x 10½ inch nonstick baking pan. bake in 350°F oven about 20 minutes or until firm.

Serves 2.

■ Not suitable to freeze.
■ Not suitable to microwave.
   Total fat: Negligible.

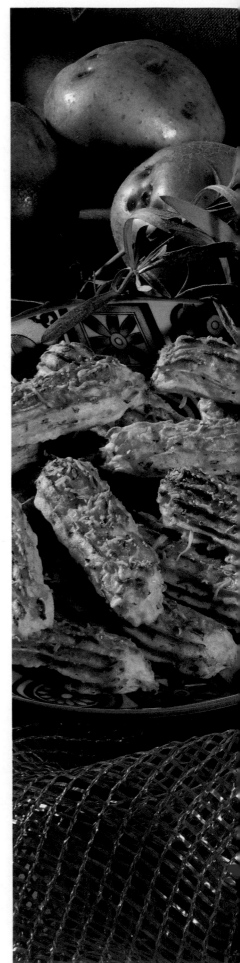

RIGHT: Clockwise from back: Cauliflower Timbales with Mustard Sauce, Baked Carrot Loaf, Golden Potato Sticks.

Desserts

♥ ♥ ♥

RASPBERRY APPLE TERRINE WITH ORANGE SAUCE

Recipe is best made a day ahead.

2¼ cups water
7oz raspberry-flavored gelatin
½ cup framboise
1 teaspoon unflavored gelatin
4 teaspoons water, extra
½lb fresh raspberries

APPLE JELLY
4 teaspoons unflavored gelatin
2 tablespoons water
2 cups clear apple juice

ORANGE SAUCE
4 teaspoons polyunsaturated margarine
¼ cup granulated sugar
1½ cups fresh orange juice
1 tablespoon cornstarch
4 teaspoons water

Wet 4½ inch x 10 inch loaf dish (6 cup capacity) with water, shake out excess water. Place strip of baking paper into dish to cover base and extend over 2 sides.

Heat 1 cup of the water in pan, add flavored gelatin, stir until dissolved. Stir in remaining water and liqueur. Sprinkle unflavored gelatin over extra water in cup, stand in pan of simmering water, stir until dissolved; stir into flavored gelatin mixture.

Pour mixture into jug, pour 1 cup mixture into prepared dish, refrigerate until set. Pour in ¼ cup apple jelly mixture, arrange half the raspberries over jelly, carefully pour ¾ cup apple jelly mixture over raspberry layer; refrigerate until set.

Continue layering and refrigerating with liqueur jelly, raspberries and apple jelly. Refrigerate several hours or overnight until set.

Unmold terrine onto plate, remove paper, serve sliced with orange sauce.

Apple Jelly: Sprinkle unflavored gelatin over water in cup, stand in small pan of simmering water, stir until dissolved. Combine with apple juice in jug.

Orange Sauce: Heat margarine in pan, stir in sugar, stir until sugar is dissolved and lightly browned. Stir in juice, stir until toffee is melted. Stir in blended cornstarch and water, stir until sauce boils and thickens. Pour into jug, cover surface, cool; refrigerate until cold.

Serves 8.

- ■ Not suitable to freeze.
- ■ Not suitable to microwave.
- ☐ Total fat: 18 grams.
- ■ Fat per serve: 2.3 grams.

RIGHT: Raspberry Apple Terrine with Orange Sauce.

96

♥ ♥ ♥
MINI ECLAIRS WITH APRICOT CREAM

You will need about 2 passion fruit for this recipe. Recipe is best made on day of serving.

CHOUX PASTRY
1 teaspoon polyunsaturated margarine
½ cup water
⅓ cup self-rising flour
2 egg whites

APRICOT CREAM
1 teaspoon unflavored gelatin
2 teaspoons water
¾ cup lowfat apricot yogurt

PASSION FRUIT SAUCE
3 tablespoons passion fruit pulp
2 teaspoons granulated sugar
1 teaspoon cornstarch
3 tablespoons water

Choux Pastry: Combine margarine and water in pan, bring to boil. Add sifted flour all at once, stirring vigorously, about 30 seconds until smooth. Transfer mixture to small bowl of electric mixer, gradually add egg whites, beating well between each addition. Mixture will separate, but will come together with further beating.

Spoon mixture into piping bag fitted with ½ inch fluted tube. Pipe 6 x 2½ inch lengths of mixture onto nonstick baking sheet. Bake in 400°F oven 10 minutes reduce heat to 350°F, bake further 15 minutes or until well browned; cool.

When eclairs are cold, cut in half, scoop out any uncooked mixture; discard. Fill eclairs with apricot cream, dust with a little sifted confectioners' sugar, if desired. Serve with sauce.

Apricot Cream: Sprinkle gelatin over water in cup, stand in small pan of simmering water; stir until dissolved. Combine yogurt and gelatin mixture in bowl, refrigerate until set.

Passion Fruit Sauce: Combine passion fruit and sugar with blended cornstarch and water in pan, stir over heat until sauce boils and thickens; cool.

Makes 6.

■ Unfilled eclairs suitable to freeze.
■ Not suitable to microwave.
□ Total fat: 5.1 grams.
■ Fat per eclair: Negligible.

♥ ♥ ♥
WHISKY ORANGES WITH TOFFEE SAUCE

Recipe is best made a day ahead.

2 oranges
3 tablespoons whisky
½ cup granulated sugar
½ cup water

Peel oranges thickly; remove all white pith from oranges. Slice oranges crossways into 4 slices; reassemble oranges. Place oranges into heatproof bowl, pour whisky over oranges.

Combine sugar and water in pan, stir over heat until sugar is dissolved. Bring to boil, boil about 10 minutes or until golden brown. Allow bubbles to subside. Drizzle one-third of the toffee on lightly oiled baking sheet to form mesh pattern; pour remaining toffee over oranges (toffee will bubble fiercely); refrigerate oranges overnight. Break toffee mesh into large pieces. Serve oranges with toffee sauce and toffee mesh.

Serves 2.

■ Not suitable to freeze.
■ Not suitable to microwave.
□ Total fat: Negligible.

♥ ♥ ♥
LINZERTORTE

Make recipe on day of serving.

¾ cup whole-wheat self-rising flour
½ teaspoon ground cinnamon
3 tablespoons dark brown sugar
4 teaspoons polyunsaturated margarine
4 teaspoons fresh lemon juice
3 tablespoons water, approximately
⅓ cup plum jam
confectioners' sugar

Sift flour, cinnamon and sugar into bowl, rub in margarine. Stir in juice with enough water to mix to firm dough. Turn dough onto lightly floured surface, knead lightly until smooth.

Roll three-quarters of the dough large enough to line base of shallow 7½ inch flan pan, spread with jam. Roll remaining dough until thin, cut into ½ inch strips, place strips over jam. Bake in 350°F oven about 40 minutes or until lightly browned. Dust with sifted confectioners' sugar; serve warm or cold.

Serves 6.

■ Suitable to freeze.
■ Not suitable to microwave.
□ Total fat: 20.8 grams.
■ Fat per serve: 3.5 grams.

ABOVE: Mini Eclairs with Apricot Cream.
RIGHT: From top: Linzertorte, Whisky Oranges with Toffee Sauce.

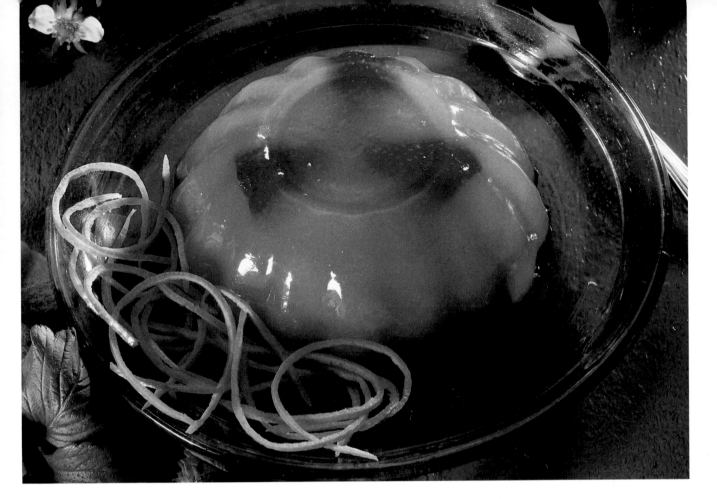

♥ ♥ ♥
APRICOT PASSION FRUIT MOUSSE

You will need about 3 passion fruit for this recipe. Recipe is best prepared several hours before serving.

30oz can apricots, drained
½ cup lowfat plain yogurt
¼ cup granulated sugar
¼ cup passion fruit pulp
4 teaspoons unflavored gelatin
3 tablespoons water

Blend or process apricots, yogurt and sugar until smooth. Transfer mixture to bowl, fold in passion fruit. Sprinkle gelatin over water in cup, stand in small pan of simmering water, stir until dissolved, cool to room temperature; do not allow to set. Combine gelatin mixture with apricot mixture, pour into 2 glasses (1 cup capacity). Refrigerate several hours or until set.

Serves 2.

■ Not suitable to freeze.
■ Not suitable to microwave.
☐ Total fat: Negligible.

♥ ♥ ♥
CHERRY SEMOLINA MOLD

Recipe is best prepared a day ahead.

16½oz can dark sweet pitted cherries
3oz package cherry-flavor gelatin
2 teaspoons unflavored gelatin
2 cups skim milk
3 tablespoons semolina
¼ cup granulated sugar
3 tablespoons unflavored gelatin, extra
¼ cup water
2 teaspoons vanilla extract
½ cup lowfat plain yogurt

Drain cherries, reserve syrup. Bring reserved syrup to boil in pan, remove from heat, stir into combined flavored gelatin and unflavored gelatin in bowl, stir until dissolved. Stir in cherries, pour into wetted mold (4 cup capacity); refrigerate until firm.

Bring milk to boil in pan, stir in semolina and sugar, stir until mixture boils and thickens; remove from heat. Sprinkle extra unflavored gelatin over water in cup, stand in small pan of simmering water, stir until dissolved.

Stir extra unflavored gelatin mixture and extract into semolina mixture; cool slightly. Stir in yogurt; cool. Pour mixture into mold over cherry layer, refrigerate until set.

Serves 4.

■ Not suitable to freeze.
■ Not suitable to microwave.
☐ Total fat: Negligible.

♥ ♥ ♥
FRESH ORANGE JELLY

Jelly can be made a day ahead. You will need about 3 oranges.

½ cup water
¼ cup granulated sugar
4 teaspoons unflavored gelatin
¼ cup cold water, extra
1⅓ cups strained fresh orange juice
¼lb strawberries, halved
1 orange, segmented

Combine water and sugar in pan, stir over heat until sugar is dissolved; remove from heat. Sprinkle gelatin over extra water in cup, stand in small pan of simmering water, stir until dissolved; cool slightly.

Combine gelatin mixture, sugar mixture and juice in bowl. Pour a little mixture into mold (3 cup capacity), place a few strawberries in mold, refrigerate until set.

Repeat layering with strawberries, orange segments and juice mixture. Refrigerate until set.

Serves 2.

■ Not suitable to freeze.
■ Not suitable to microwave.
☐ Total fat: Negligible.

LEFT: From top: Apricot Passion Fruit Mousse, Cherry Semolina Mold.
ABOVE: Fresh Orange Jelly.

♥ ♥ ♥
APPLE AND PEAR STRUDEL

Make strudel close to serving time.

1 apple, sliced
1 pear, sliced
4 teaspoons granulated sugar
¼ teaspoon grated lemon zest
⅛ teaspoon ground cinnamon
3 tablespoons water
3 sheets phyllo pastry

CUSTARD SAUCE
2 teaspoons custard powder
1 tablespoon granulated sugar
¾ cup skim milk

Combine apple, pear, sugar, zest, cinnamon and water in pan, cook until fruit is soft; cool. Layer pastry sheets together, fold in half, spoon fruit mixture evenly along center of pastry, fold in ends, fold sides over fruit.

Place strudel, with folded edge down, onto baking paper-covered baking sheet, bake in 400°F oven 7 minutes, turn strudel over, bake further 7 minutes or until well browned. Serve with sauce.

Custard Sauce: Combine custard powder and sugar in pan, gradually stir in milk. Stir over medium heat until sauce boils and thickens.

Serves 2.

- ■ Not suitable to freeze.
- ■ Not suitable to microwave.
- ■ Total fat: Negligible.

♥ ♥ ♥
BUTTERMILK PANCAKES WITH GOLDEN PEARS

Recipe best made just before serving.

BUTTERMILK PANCAKES
1 cup self-rising flour
1 cup buttermilk
¼ cup skim milk
1 egg white

GOLDEN PEARS
2 pears, halved
¼ cup honey
1 cup water
4 teaspoons lemon juice
1 tablespoon cornstarch
4 teaspoons water, extra

Buttermilk Pancakes: Sift flour into bowl, gradually stir in combined milks to make a smooth batter. Beat egg white until soft peaks form, fold lightly into batter.

Pour ½ cup batter mixture into heated nonstick skillet. When bubbles appear, turn pancake, cook until lightly browned underneath, remove from skillet; keep warm. Repeat with remaining batter. Serve pancakes topped with golden pears and syrup.

Golden Pears: Place pears into pan with honey, water and juice, bring to boil, simmer, uncovered, until pears are just tender. Remove pears from syrup; reserve syrup. Slice pears lengthways; serve over pancakes.

Stir blended cornstarch and extra water into pan, stir over heat until mixture boils and thickens. Serve sauce over pears.

Serves 4.

- ■ Not suitable to freeze.
- ■ Not suitable to microwave.
- □ Total fat: 7.5 grams.
- ■ Fat per serve: 1.9 grams.

RIGHT: From top: Apple and Pear Strudel, Buttermilk Pancakes with Golden Pears.

♥ ♥ ♥
BLUEBERRY TOFU ICE CREAM

Ice cream can be made 3 days ahead.

14oz can blueberries
10½oz package soft tofu
½ cup skim milk
½ cup granulated sugar

Blend or process undrained blueberries, tofu, milk and sugar until smooth. Pour mixture into large loaf pan, cover, freeze several hours or until firm.

Spoon mixture into bowl, beat with electric mixer until smooth. Return mixture to pan, cover; freeze until firm.

Serves 4.

- ■ Not suitable to microwave.
- □ Total fat: 14.9 grams.
- ■ Fat per serve: 3.7 grams.

♥ ♥ ♥
SNOW EGGS WITH COFFEE CREAM

Make eggs just before serving. Coffee cream can be prepared a day ahead.

2 egg whites
3 tablespoons granulated sugar
1 cup skim milk

COFFEE CREAM
2 teaspoons cornstarch
4 teaspoons granulated sugar
1 cup skim milk
2 teaspoons coffee and chicory extract
2 teaspoons brandy

Beat egg whites in small bowl until soft peaks form. Add sugar, beat until sugar is dissolved. Bring milk to boil in shallow pan, reduce to simmer.

Using 2 dessertspoons, shape egg white mixture into ovals. Lower ovals into milk, cook 1 minute each side, do not allow to boil or ovals will break up. Remove from pan with slotted spoon; drain. Serve snow eggs with coffee cream.

Coffee Cream: Combine cornstarch and sugar in pan, gradually stir in milk. Stir over heat until sauce boils and thickens. Remove from heat, Stir in extract and brandy; cool.

Serves 2.

- ■ Not suitable to freeze.
- ■ Not suitable to microwave.
- □ Total fat: Negligible.

♥ ♥ ♥
PINEAPPLE SHERBET

Sherbet can be made 2 weeks ahead.

3lb fresh pineapple
½ cup water
¼ cup granulated sugar
4 teaspoons lemon juice
1 egg white

Peel and chop pineapple (you should have about 1¼lb pineapple flesh).

Combine water and sugar in pan, stir over heat until sugar is dissolved. Bring to boil, simmer 1 minute; cool. Blend or process sugar syrup, pineapple and juice until combined. Pour mixture into shallow baking pan, cover, freeze several hours or until firm.

Place mixture into large bowl of electric mixer or food processor with egg white; beat until creamy. Return mixture to pan, cover, freeze until firm. Allow to soften in refrigerator 15 minutes before serving.

Serves 4.

- ■ Not suitable to microwave.
- □ Total fat: Negligible.

♥ ♥ ♥
RED GRAPE AND PORT GRANITA

Recipe can be made a week ahead.

1lb dark red grapes
2 cups water
3 tablespoons port wine
4 teaspoons honey
1 teaspoon grated lemon zest
½ teaspoon dark soy sauce
1 egg white

Combine grapes and water in pan, bring to boil, simmer, covered, about 1 hour or until grapes are soft; cool. Blend or process mixture until smooth, push mixture through sieve, discard skins and seeds.

Combine grape mixture, port wine, honey, zest and sauce. Pour into large loaf pan, cover, freeze until just firm. Process granita until smooth, add egg white with motor operating, process until smooth and pale. Return mixture to pan, cover, freeze until firm.

Serves 2.

- ■ Not suitable to microwave.
- □ Total fat: Negligible.

ABOVE: Snow Eggs with Coffee Cream.
RIGHT: Clockwise from back: Blueberry Tofu Ice Cream, Pineapple Sherbet, Red Grape and Port Granita.

Baking

♥ ♥ ♥
CHILI ONION TWIST

Make bread on day of serving.

1 package (¼oz) active dry yeast
1 teaspoon granulated sugar
¾ cup warm water
2¼ cups whole-wheat flour
½ teaspoon salt
3 tablespoons chopped fresh chives
1 onion, chopped
3 green onions, chopped
⅓ cup sweet chili sauce

Combine yeast, sugar and water in bowl cover, stand bowl in warm place about 10 minutes or until frothy.

Sift flour and salt into large bowl, make well in center, stir in yeast mixture and chives, mix to a soft dough. Turn dough onto floured surface, knead about 7 minutes until smooth and elastic.

Return dough to lightly oiled bowl, cover, stand in warm place about 45 minutes or until dough is doubled in size.

Knead dough on lightly floured surface until smooth. Roll dough evenly to 8 inch x 24 inch rectangle, spread with combined onion, green onions and sauce, leaving ¾ inch border on 1 side. Roll dough up from covered long side like a jelly-roll. Holding ends together, twist roll twice, place onto baking paper-covered baking sheet. Stand, uncovered, 20 minutes. Prick with skewer. Bake in 375˚F oven about 30 minutes or until well browned and cooked through.

Serves 6.

■ Suitable to freeze.
■ Not suitable to microwave.
□ Total fat: 8.4 grams.
■ Fat per serve: 1.4 grams.

♥ ♥ ♥
BAPS

Make baps close to serving time.

2 packages (½oz) active dry yeast
2 teaspoons granulated sugar
⅔ cup warm water
⅔ cup warm buttermilk
3½ cups all-purpose flour
¼ teaspoon salt
4 teaspoons polyunsaturated margarine

Cream yeast and sugar in bowl, stir in water and buttermilk. Cover, stand bowl in warm place about 10 minutes or until mixture is frothy.

Sift flour and salt into bowl, rub in margarine; make well in center. Stir in yeast mixture, mix to soft dough.

Turn dough onto floured surface, knead about 7 minutes or until dough is smooth and elastic.

Return dough to lightly oiled bowl, cover, stand bowl in warm place about 45 minutes or until doubled in size.

Turn dough onto lightly floured surface, knead until smooth. Divide dough evenly into 12 portions, shape each portion into a round, place each round onto baking paper-covered baking sheet; press finger firmly into center of each round. Cover, stand in warm place about 20 minutes or until rounds are doubled in size. Bake in 375˚F oven about 15 minutes or until lightly browned and cooked through.

Makes 12.

■ Suitable to freeze.
■ Not suitable to microwave.
□ Total fat: 30.2 grams.
■ Fat per bap: 2.5 grams.

♥ ♥ ♥
PUMPKIN SQUASH DAMPER

You will need to cook about 1lb pumpkin squash for this recipe. Best made close to serving time.

3 cups self-rising flour
2 teaspoons polyunsaturated margarine
1½ cups cooked mashed pumpkin squash
4 teaspoons water, approximately

Sift flour into bowl, rub in margarine. Stir in squash and enough water to mix to a sticky dough. Turn dough onto lightly floured surface, knead until smooth. Place damper on nonstick baking sheet, pat out to 10 inch round, cut ½ inch deep cross in surface.

Bake in 400°F oven 10 minutes, reduce heat to 350°F, bake further 20 minutes or until golden brown and cooked through.

Serves 8.

- ▪ Suitable to freeze.
- ▪ Not suitable to microwave.
- ▫ Total fat: 16.6 grams.
- ▪ Fat per serve: 2 grams.

♥ ♥ ♥
WHOLE-WHEAT CRACKERS

Crackers can be made 3 days ahead.

½ cup whole-wheat flour
¼ cup all-purpose four
4 teaspoons polyunsaturated margarine
¼ cup grated Parmesan cheese
⅛ teaspoon cayenne pepper
1 egg white, lightly beaten
3 tablespoons water, approximately

Sift flours into bowl, rub in margarine, stir in cheese and pepper. Stir in egg white with enough water to make ingredients cling together. Turn dough onto lightly floured surface, knead until smooth. Roll dough evenly into 7 inch x 14 inch rectangle, fold in half lengthways, repeat rolling and folding.

Roll dough out until ⅛ inch thick, cut into 18 rounds using 2½ inch cutter. Place rounds onto baking paper-covered baking sheet, bake in 375°F oven about 12 minutes or until golden brown; cool on baking sheet.

Makes 18.

- ▪ Suitable to freeze.
- ▪ Not suitable to microwave.
- ▫ Total fat: 30 grams.
- ▪ Fat per cracker: 1.6 grams.

LEFT: Clockwise from back left: Pumpkin Squash Damper, Whole-Wheat Crackers, Baps, Chili Onion Twist.

surface until smooth. Roll dough evenly to 8 inch x 16 inch rectangle.

Sprinkle fig mixture over dough, roll up dough from long side; cut into 12 slices.

Place slices in prepared pan, bake in 400°F oven about 20 minutes or until cooked through. Stand 5 minutes before turning onto wire rack to cool. Drizzle with frosting when cold.

Orange Frosting: Sift confectioners' sugar into bowl, stir in zest and enough juice to give a pouring consistency.

Makes 12.

- Suitable to freeze.
- Not suitable to microwave.
- Total fat: 25.7 grams.
- Fat per pinwheel: 2 grams.

♥ ♥

CUSTARD TARTS WITH LOWFAT SWEET PASTRY

Tarts can be made a day ahead.

LOWFAT SWEET PASTRY
2 teaspoons polyunsaturated margarine
4 teaspoons granulated sugar
¾ cup self-rising flour
4 teaspoons custard powder
¼ cup water

CUSTARD FILLING
2 teaspoons unflavored gelatin
4 teaspoons water
4 teaspoons granulated sugar
4 teaspoons custard powder
¾ cup skim milk
1 teaspoon vanilla extract

Lowfat Sweet Pastry: Cream margarine and sugar in bowl with wooden spoon until well combined. Stir in sifted flour and custard powder with water in 2 batches. Knead dough on lightly floured surface until smooth. Divide dough into 2 portions, press dough with fingers evenly over bases and sides of 2 x 4½ inch nonstick pie tins.

Bake in 350°F oven about 15 minutes or until lightly browned, cool in tins. Remove pastry cases from tins, fill with custard filling, sprinkle with a little nutmeg, if desired. Refrigerate until custard is set.

Custard Filling: Sprinkle gelatin over water in a cup, stand in small pan of simmering water, stir until dissolved. Combine sugar with custard powder in pan, gradually stir in milk, stir over heat until mixture boils and thickens. Stir in extract and gelatin mixture.

Makes 2.

- Not suitable to freeze.
- Not suitable to microwave.
- Total fat: 10.7 grams.
- Fat per serve: 5.4 grams.

♥ ♥ ♥
CRANBERRY MUFFINS

Muffins can be made a day ahead.

1 cup whole-wheat self-rising flour
¾ cup oat bran
⅓ cup granulated sugar
½ teaspoon ground cinnamon
⅔ cup cranberry sauce
1 egg white
4 teaspoons polyunsaturated margarine, melted
⅔ cup buttermilk

Line 12 x ⅓ cup muffin tins with paper baking cups. Combine sifted flour, bran, sugar and cinnamon in bowl. Stir in sauce, egg white, margarine and buttermilk. Spoon mixture into prepared tins, bake in 350°F oven about 25 minutes or until firm.

Makes 12.

- Suitable to freeze.
- Not suitable to microwave.
- Total fat: 31.6 grams.
- Fat per muffin: 2.6 grams.

♥ ♥ ♥
FIG AND ORANGE PINWHEELS

Recipe can be made 3 hours ahead.

1¾ cups (½lb) dried figs, chopped
¼ cup fresh orange juice
3 cups self-rising flour
4 teaspoons polyunsaturated margarine
4 teaspoons grated orange zest
1 cup skim milk
¼ cup water, approximately

ORANGE FROSTING
1 cup confectioners' sugar
1 teaspoon grated orange zest
3 tablespoons fresh orange juice, approximately

Combine figs and juice in bowl, stand several hours or overnight.

Lightly grease deep 9 inch round baking pan, line base with baking paper. Sift flour into bowl, rub in margarine. Stir in zest and milk with enough water to mix to a firm dough, knead on lightly floured

♥ ♥ ♥

OATY RAISIN COOKIES

Cookies can be made 3 days ahead.

1½ cups old-fashioned oats
½ cup golden raisins
¼ cup self-rising flour
¼ cup dark brown sugar
2 egg whites
3 tablespoons honey
4 teaspoons polyunsaturated
**   margarine, melted**

Combine oats, golden raisins, sifted flour and sugar in bowl. Stir in combined egg whites, honey and margarine. Drop heaped tablespoons of mixture about 1¼ inches apart on baking paper-covered baking sheets, press with fork. Bake in 350°F oven about 15 minutes or until golden brown. Lift onto wire rack to cool.

Makes 16.
- ■ Suitable to freeze.
- ■ Not suitable to microwave.
- □ Total fat: 29 grams.
- ■ Fat per cookie: 1.8 grams.

♥ ♥ ♥

MAPLE SYRUP AND PECAN CAKE

Cake can be made 4 days ahead.

1 cup bran cereal
½ cup dark brown sugar
1½ cups skim milk
¼ cup water
¾ cup golden raisins
¼ cup chopped pecans
½ cup self-rising flour
1 cup whole-wheat self-rising flour
2 teaspoons mixed water

SYRUP
½ cup maple syrup
3 tablespoons water

Lightly grease 5½ inch x 8½ inch loaf pan, line base and sides with baking paper. Combine bran cereal, sugar, milk, water, golden raisins and nuts in bowl, stand 10 minutes. Stir in sifted flours and spice; mix well.

Spread mixture into prepared pan, bake in 325°F oven about 1¼ hours or until firm. Stand cake in pan 5 minutes, turn onto wire rack; stand rack on tray. Pour hot syrup over cake.

Syrup: Combine syrup and water in pan, stir until heated through.

Serves 10.
- ■ Suitable to freeze.
- ■ Not suitable to microwave.
- □ Total fat: 28 grams.
- ■ Fat per slice: 2.8 grams.

LEFT: Custard Tarts with Lowfat Sweet Pastry.
BELOW: Clockwise from back left: Cranberry Muffins, Oaty Raisin Cookies, Fig and Orange Pinwheels, Maple Syrup and Pecan Cake.

BANANA NUT LOAF

You need 2 large over-ripe bananas.
Loaf can be made a day ahead.

1/4 **cup chopped hazelnuts**
1/4 **cup chopped pitted dates**
2 1/4 **cups self-rising flour**
1/3 **cup dark brown sugar**
1 **cup mashed banana**
1/2 **cup buttermilk**
1/4 **cup nonfat dry milk**
3 **tablespoons corn syrup**
2 **egg whites**

Lightly grease 6 inch x 10 inch loaf pan, line base with baking paper. Combine nuts, dates, sifted flour and sugar in bowl; stir in banana. Gradually stir in combined buttermilk, dry milk, syrup and egg whites until combined. Pour mixture into prepared pan. Bake in 350°F oven about 45 minutes or until firm.

Serves 12.

■ Suitable to freeze.
■ Not suitable to microwave.
  Total fat: 19.4 grams.
■ Fat per slice: 1.6 grams.

APRICOT PRUNE LOAF

Loaf can be made 2 days ahead.

1/2 **cup dried apricots**
1 1/4 **cups water**
1 **over-ripe banana**
2 **cups whole-wheat self-rising flour**
1/4 **cup granulated sugar**
1/2 **teaspoon ground cinnamon**
2 **tablespoons polyunsaturated margarine**
1/2 **cup pitted prunes, chopped**
1 **egg, lightly beaten**

Lightly grease 5½ inch x 8½ inch loaf pan, line with baking paper. Combine apricots and water in pan, bring to boil, simmer 5 minutes; cool to room temperature. Blend or process apricot mixture and banana until smooth.

Sift flour, sugar and cinnamon into bowl, rub in margarine. Stir in prunes, egg and apricot mixture. Spoon mixture into prepared pan, bake in 350°F oven about 45 minutes or until firm. Stand 5 minutes before turning onto wire rack to cool.

Serves 10.

- ■ Suitable to freeze.
- ■ Not suitable to microwave.
- ☐ Total fat: 36 grams.
- ■ Fat per slice: 3.6 grams.

♥ ♥ ♥
APPLE GINGERROOT SHORTCAKE

You will need about 2 passion fruit. Recipe can be made a day ahead.

PASTRY
1¼ cups self-rising flour
4 teaspoons cornstarch
3 tablespoons granulated sugar
3 tablespoons polyunsaturated margarine
2 egg whites
1 teaspoon fresh lemon juice, approximately

APPLE GINGERROOT FILLING
15oz can pie apples
4 teaspoons passion fruit pulp
1 teaspoon finely chopped glace gingerroot
1 teaspoon grated lemon zest

PASSION FRUIT FROSTING
I cup confectioners' sugar
1 teaspoon polyunsaturated margarine
4 teaspoons passion fruit pulp
1 teaspoon skim milk, approximately

Pastry: Lightly grease shallow 8 inch round baking pan, line base with baking paper. Sift dry ingredients into bowl, rub in margarine, stir in egg whites with enough juice to make ingredients cling together (or process all ingredients until mixture forms ball), cover, refrigerate 30 minutes.

Roll three-quarters of the pastry between 2 pieces of baking paper until large enough to line base and side of prepared pan, lift into pan, trim edges. Spread filling over base, fold pastry edge over filling, lightly brush edge with water. Roll out remaining pastry to an 8 inch round, place over filling, press edges to seal. Bake in 350°F oven about 40 minutes or until lightly browned. Cool on wire rack. Spread with frosting.

Apple Gingerroot Filling: Combine all ingredients in bowl; mix well.

Passion Fruit Frosting: Sift confectioners' sugar into heatproof bowl, stir in margarine and passion fruit, then enough milk to make a stiff paste. Stir over hot water until frosting is spreadable.

Serves 10.

- ■ Not suitable to freeze.
- ■ Not suitable to microwave.
- ☐ Total fat: 43 grams.
- ■ Fat per serve: 4.3 grams.

LEFT: From top: Banana Nut Loaf, Apricot Prune Loaf.
ABOVE: Apple Gingerroot Shortcake.

♥ ♥ ♥
PEACH AND YOGURT CAKE

Cake is best made just before serving; serve warm.

2 cups whole-wheat self-rising flour
½ cup granulated sugar
2 teaspoons ground cinnamon
1 teaspoon ground gingerroot
½ teaspoon ground allspice
1 teaspoon vanilla extract
3½oz no-cholesterol egg substitute
½ cup water
½ cup lowfat plain yogurt
4 teaspoons olive oil
13oz can pie peaches

Lightly grease 9 inch square baking pan, line base with baking paper. Sift flour, sugar and spices into bowl. Add extract, egg substitute, water, yogurt and oil, beat with electric mixer until smooth.

Reserve quarter of mixture. Spread remaining mixture into prepared pan. Top with peaches, spread with reserved mixture. Bake in 350°F oven about 45 minutes or lightly browned. Stand 5 minutes, turn onto wire rack to cool.

Serves 12.

■ Suitable to freeze.
■ Not suitable to microwave.
   Total fat: 36.8 grams.
■ Fat per serve: 3 grams.

♥ ♥ ♥
FRUITY COOKIES

Cookies can be made 3 days ahead.

1 cup whole-wheat self-rising flour
½ teaspoon ground cinnamon
½ teaspoon ground nutmeg
3 tablespoons dark brown sugar
4 teaspoons finely chopped
   dried apricots
4 teaspoons finely chopped
   dried apples
4 teaspoons golden raisins
4 teaspoons olive oil
3½oz no-cholesterol egg substitute
¼ cup skim milk

Sift dry ingredients into bowl, stir in fruit; make well in center. Add oil, egg substitute and milk, stir until combined. Place 2 heaped tablespoons mixture about 2 inches apart onto nonstick baking sheets. Bake in 375°F oven about 15 minutes or until lightly browned; cool on sheets.

Makes 8.

■ Suitable to freeze.
■ Not suitable to microwave.
   Total fat: 33 grams.
■ Fat per cookie: 4 grams.

♥ ♥ ♥
APPLE CINNAMON COOKIES WITH PASSION FRUIT FROSTING

You will need about 2 passion fruit.
Cookies can be made 2 weeks ahead.

1 cup self-rising flour
½ teaspoon ground cinnamon
3 tablespoons polyunsaturated
  margarine
1 apple, grated
⅓ cup fresh orange juice
½ cup old-fashioned oats
3 tablespoons honey

PASSION FRUIT FROSTING
1 cup confectioners' sugar
4 teaspoons passion fruit pulp
1 teaspoon polyunsaturated
  margarine
1 teaspoon skim milk, approximately

Sift flour and cinnamon into bowl, rub in margarine. Stir in apple, juice, oats and honey. Drop heaped tablespoons of mixture 2 inches apart onto nonstick baking sheet, bake in 350°F oven about 40 minutes or until lightly browned. Lift cookies onto wire rack to cool. Spread cold cookies with passion fruit frosting.

Passion Fruit Frosting: Sift confectioners' sugar into heatproof bowl, stir in passion fruit and margarine, then enough milk to make a stiff paste. Stir over hot water until spreadable.

Makes 24.

- Suitable to freeze.
- Not suitable to microwave.
  Total fat: 46.6 grams.
- Fat per cookie: 1.9 grams.

LEFT: Clockwise from back: Peach and Yogurt Cake, Apple Cinnamon Cookies with Passion Fruit Frosting, Fruity Cookies.

Drinks

♥ ♥ ♥
PEACH SUNRISE

Prepare drink 3 hours ahead.

⅔ cup boiling water
1 tea bag
16oz can peaches
⅓ cup lowfat plain yogurt
2 teaspoons grenadine syrup

Pour boiling water over tea bag in cup, stand 5 minutes, discard tea bag; cool tea to room temperature; do not refrigerate tea.

Drain peaches, reserve ⅓ cup peach liquid. Blend or process peaches, reserved liquid, tea and yogurt until smooth. Swirl grenadine into 2 glasses, pour in peach mixture.

Serves 2.

Total fat: Negligible.

LEFT: From left: Honeydew Dream, Peach Sunrise, Pineapple Wine Whip.
ABOVE: Banana Raisin Whip.

♥ ♥ ♥
HONEYDEW DREAM

Make recipe just before serving.

½lb honeydew melon, chopped
4 teaspoons nonfat dry milk
4 teaspoons fresh lime juice
3 tablespoons buttermilk
1 teaspoon sugar
6 ice cubes

Blend or process all ingredients until smooth and creamy.

Serves 2.

Total fat: Negligible.

♥ ♥ ♥
PINEAPPLE WINE WHIP

Make recipe just before serving.

1lb pineapple
⅓ cup granulated sugar
1 cup sweet white wine
1 tablespoon coconut extract
⅓ cup water

Chop pineapple, spread pineapple on freezer tray; partially freeze. Blend or process pineapple, sugar, wine, extract and water until smooth.

Serves 4.

Total fat: Negligible.

♥ ♥ ♥
BANANA RAISIN WHIP

Make recipe just before serving.

1 cup skim milk
4 teaspoons fresh lemon juice
1 banana, chopped
3 tablespoons golden raisins
3 tablespoons wheatgerm
2 teaspoons honey
¼ teaspoon ground cinnamon

Blend or process all ingredients until smooth and creamy.

Serves 2.

Total fat: 3 grams.
■ Fat per serve: 1.5 grams.

♥ ♥ ♥
ICED GINGER COFFEE

Make recipe just before serving.

2 teaspoons dry instant coffee
1 cup boiling water
¾ cup skim milk
¼ cup dry ginger ale

Combine coffee and water in jug; cool, then refrigerate until cold. Stir in remaining ingredients. Serve with ice.

Serves 2.

Total fat: Negligible.

♥ ♥ ♥
MANGO SMOOTHIE

Make recipe just before serving.

1 large mango, chopped
1 cup skim milk
½ cup fresh orange juice
4 teaspoons sugar

Blend or process all ingredients until smooth and creamy.

Serves 2.

Total fat: Negligible.

♥ ♥ ♥
APRICOT TROPICANA

Make recipe just before serving.

16oz can apricot halves, drained
1 apple, chopped
1 banana, chopped
1 mango, chopped
1 cup lemonade
4 teaspoons white rum
4 teaspoons gin

Blend or process all ingredients until well combined.

Serves 4.

Total fat: Negligible.

♥ ♥ ♥
TOMATO SPARKLE

Make recipe just before serving.

2 tomatoes, peeled, chopped
1 teaspoon Worcestershire sauce
4 teaspoons sugar
4 teaspoons chopped fresh mint
1½ cups carbonated mineral water
red food coloring

Blend or process tomatoes, sauce and sugar, until well combined. Combine tomato mixture, mint and mineral water in jug. Tint with coloring, if desired.

Serves 2.

Total fat: Negligible.

ABOVE: Iced Ginger Coffee.
RIGHT: From left: Mango Smoothie, Apricot Tropicana, Tomato Sparkle.

Light lunch for

10

MENU
Layered Vegetable Soy Bean Loaf
Honeyed Chicken Stir-Fry
Triple Rice Salad with Citrus Plum Dressing
Potato Tomato Salad with Garlic Yogurt Cream
Fruit Platter with Red Currant Sauce
Pavlova with Peach Custard

Your guests will enjoy lots to eat with these
light but satisfying dishes – even 2 luscious
desserts! Fat per person is about
9 grams over all courses.

♥ ♥ ♥
LAYERED VEGETABLE SOY BEAN LOAF

Make recipe just before serving.

15oz can soy beans, rinsed, drained
1 cup seasoned stuffing mix
3 egg whites
2 cloves garlic, minced
½ teaspoon chili powder

TOPPING
2 carrots, grated
2 zucchini, grated
2 green onions, chopped
½lb pumpkin squash, grated
2 potatoes, grated
½ cup lowfat cottage cheese
7oz no-cholesterol egg substitute
⅓ cup skim milk

Line 5½ inch x 8½ inch loaf pan with
baking paper. Blend or process beans,
stuffing mix, egg whites, garlic and chili
until well combined. Spread mixture into
prepared pan, bake in 350˚F oven about
20 minutes or until firm; cool.

Spread topping over loaf in pan, bake in
350˚F oven about 30 minutes or until firm
and lightly browned. Serve warm or cold.
Topping: Combine all ingredients in bowl;
mix well.

Serves 10.

- ■ Not suitable to freeze.
- ■ Not suitable to microwave.
   Total fat: 43.5 grams.
- ■ Fat per serve: 4.4 grams.

*LEFT: Back, from left: Pavlova with Peach Custard, Triple Rice Salad
with Citrus Plum Dressing, Potato Tomato Salad with Garlic Yogurt
Cream. Front, from left: Fruit Platter with Red Currant Sauce, Honeyed
Chicken Stir-Fry, Layered Vegetable Soy Bean Loaf.*

ABOVE: From top: Honeyed Chicken Stir-Fry, Fruit Platter with Red Currant Sauce.

♥ ♥ ♥
HONEYED CHICKEN STIR-FRY

Cook recipe just before serving.

2½lb boneless, skinless chicken breasts, sliced
⅓ cup reduced sodium soy sauce
½ cup honey
2 cloves garlic, minced
1 teaspoon chopped fresh gingerroot
1 red bell pepper, chopped
1lb broccoli, chopped
2 x 15oz cans baby corn, drained
½ medium cabbage, shredded

Combine chicken, sauce, honey, garlic and gingerroot in bowl, refrigerate several hours or overnight.

Cook mixture in nonstick wok or skillet until chicken is just cooked through; remove mixture from wok. Add pepper, broccoli and corn to wok, stir-fry about 5 minutes or until broccoli is just tender. Stir in chicken and cabbage, stir-fry until cabbage is just wilted.

Serves 10.

■ Not suitable to freeze.
■ Not suitable to microwave.
□ Total fat: 27 grams.
■ Fat per serve: 2.7 grams.

120

♥ ♥ ♥
TRIPLE RICE SALAD WITH CITRUS PLUM DRESSING

Recipe can be made a day ahead. Salad can be served hot or cold.

1½ cups (10oz) wild rice
8 cups water
5 small yellow squash, sliced
1½ cups (10oz) brown rice
2 cups (½lb) frozen peas
2 carrots
1 cup basmati rice

CITRUS PLUM DRESSING
¼ cup fresh lemon juice
3 tablespoons fresh lime juice
⅓ cup fresh orange juice
2 teaspoons sambal oelek
1 teaspoon light olive oil
3 tablespoons plum jam, sieved
¼ cup chopped fresh chives

Combine wild rice with 3 cups of the water in pan, bring to boil, simmer, covered, about 20 minutes or until rice is tender and almost all liquid is absorbed. Stir in zucchini, cook, covered, further 5 minutes or until all liquid is absorbed. Stir in one-third of the dressing.

Combine brown rice with 3 cups of remaining water in pan, bring to boil, simmer, covered, about 20 minutes or until rice is tender and almost all liquid is absorbed. Stir in peas, cook, covered, further 5 minutes or until all liquid is absorbed. Stir in half remaining dressing.

Cut carrots into thin strips. Combine basmati rice with remaining water in pan, simmer, covered, about 12 minutes or until rice is tender and almost all liquid is absorbed. Stir in carrots, cook, covered, about 5 minutes or until all liquid is absorbed. Stir in remaining dressing.

Citrus Plum Dressing: Blend or process juices, sambal oelek, oil and jam until smooth; stir in chives.

Serves 10.

- ■ Not suitable to freeze.
- ■ Not suitable to microwave.
- ☐ Total fat: 11.8 grams.
- ■ Fat per serve: 1.2 grams.

♥ ♥ ♥
POTATO TOMATO SALAD WITH GARLIC YOGURT CREAM

Recipe can be made a day ahead. Salad can be served warm or cold.

4lb baby potatoes, halved
1lb cherry tomatoes

GARLIC YOGURT CREAM
3 tablespoons nonfat dry milk
⅓ cup lowfat plain yogurt
⅓ cup buttermilk
3 tablespoons no-added-salt tomato paste
3 tablespoons fresh lemon juice
3 tablespoons chopped fresh parsley
3 tablespoons chopped fresh basil
2 cloves garlic, minced

Boil, steam or microwave potatoes until tender; drain. Combine potatoes and tomatoes in serving bowl; add dressing just before serving.

Garlic Yogurt Cream: Blend or process dry milk, yogurt, buttermilk, paste and juice until smooth. Stir in herbs and garlic.

Serves 10.

- ■ Not suitable to freeze.
- ■ Not suitable to microwave.
- ☐ Total fat: 1.5 grams.
- ■ Fat per serve: Negligible.

♥ ♥ ♥
FRUIT PLATTER WITH RED CURRANT SAUCE

You will need about 6 passion fruit for this recipe. Prepare fruit close to serving time. Sauce can be made a day ahead.

2 mangoes, sliced
1lb strawberries
½ canteloupe, sliced
4 oranges, segmented
2 pears, sliced
2 apples, sliced
2 bananas, sliced
6 kiwifruit, sliced
½lb blueberries
½ cup passion fruit pulp

RED CURRANT SAUCE
7oz fresh or frozen red currants
1½ cups water
¼ cup sugar
4 teaspoons cornstarch
4 teaspoons water, extra
3 tablespoons Grand Marnier

Arrange fruit on platter; serve with sauce.

Red Currant Sauce: Combine red currants, water and sugar in pan, bring to boil, simmer, covered, 3 minutes. Blend or process until smooth, strain; discard seeds. Return liquid to pan, stir in blended cornstarch and extra water, stir until sauce boils and thickens. Stir in liqueur.

Serves 10.

- ■ Not suitable to freeze.
- ■ Suitable to microwave.
- ☐ Total fat: Negligible.

♥ ♥ ♥
PAVLOVA WITH PEACH CUSTARD

Pavlova and custard can be made a day ahead. Assemble pavlova 3 hours before serving.

6 egg whites
1½ cups granulated sugar

PEACH CUSTARD
½ cup granulated sugar
½ cup cornstarch
¼ cup custard powder
2¼ cups skim milk
3 x 16oz cans peaches in natural juice, well drained

Mark 11 inch circle on baking paper-covered baking sheet. Beat egg whites in large bowl with electric mixer until soft peaks form. Gradually add sugar, beat until dissolved between each addition.

Spread half the egg white mixture evenly over circle on baking sheet, pipe remaining mixture around edge. Bake in 250°F oven about 1½ hours or until dry to touch. Turn oven off; cool pavlova in oven with door ajar.

Fill cold pavlova with custard; decorate with extra peaches, if desired.

Peach Custard: Combine sugar, cornstarch and custard powder in pan, gradually stir in milk. Stir over heat until custard boils and thickens, simmer 1 minute; cool. Blend or process peaches and custard until smooth.

Serves 10.

- ■ Not suitable to freeze.
- ■ Not suitable to microwave.
- ☐ Total fat: Negligible.

Easy Dinner Party for 6

MENU
Jellied Beets with Chive Dressing
Lamb Noisettes with Leek and Bell Pepper Sauce
Mixed Green Salad
Sorbet Pastry Rings with Butterscotch Sauce

Both the entree and the dessert
are made ahead, leaving you
only the main course to prepare just
before serving. Fat per person
is about 18 grams over all courses.

♥ ♥ ♥
JELLIED BEETS WITH CHIVE DRESSING

Recipe can be made a day ahead.

15oz fresh beets
1 cup fresh orange juice
1 cup cranberry jelly
4 teaspoons unflavored gelatin
3 tablespoons water

CHIVE DRESSING
4 teaspoons olive oil
4 teaspoons fresh lemon juice
2 teaspoons white wine vinegar
2 teaspoons chopped fresh chives
¼ teaspoon cracked black peppercorns
¼ teaspoon seeded mustard

Wash beets, cut off leafy tops. Cook beets in pan of boiling water about 1 hour or until skin can be removed easily; drain. Remove skin; chop beets finely.

Heat juice and jelly in pan, stir until jelly is dissolved. Sprinkle gelatin over water in cup, stand in small pan of simmering water, stir until dissolved. Stir gelatin into juice mixture; stir in beets. Pour into 6 wetted molds (½ cup capacity), refrigerate several hours or overnight until set. Unmold jellies onto plates, serve with chive dressing.

Chive Dressing: Combine all ingredients in jar; shake well.

Serves 6.

■ Not suitable to freeze.
■ Not suitable to microwave.
□ Total fat: 18 grams.
■ Fat per serve: 3 grams.

LEFT: Clockwise from front: Jellied Beets with Chive Dressing, Mixed Green Salad, Sorbet Pastry Rings with Butterscotch Sauce, Lamb Noisettes with Leek and Bell Pepper Sauce.

♥ ♥

LAMB NOISETTES WITH LEEK AND BELL PEPPER SAUCE

Cook noisettes just before serving. Sauce can be made 3 hours ahead.

12 x 3oz lamb noisettes
½ cup cooked brown rice
4 green onions, chopped
2 teaspoons chopped fresh thyme

LEEK AND BELL PEPPER SAUCE
4 teaspoons olive oil
1 leek, sliced
1 carrot, finely chopped
1 red bell pepper, chopped
1 vegetable bouillon cube, crumbled
2 cups water
4 teaspoons chopped fresh mint
1 teaspoon chopped fresh thyme
2 green onions, chopped
1 tablespoon cornstarch
¼ cup water, extra

Trim all visible fat from noisettes. Cut a deep pocket in top of each noisette. Combine rice, onions and thyme in bowl. Fill pockets with rice mixture, secure with toothpicks. Broil noisettes until cooked as desired. Serve noisettes with leek and bell pepper sauce.
Leek and Bell Pepper Sauce: Heat oil in pan, add leek, cook, stirring, over heat until leek is soft. Stir in carrot, pepper, combined bouillon cube and water, bring to boil, simmer, covered, about 7 minutes or until vegetables are tender. Stir in herbs, onions, blended cornstarch and extra water. Stir over high heat until sauce boils and thickens.

Serves 6.

■ Not suitable to freeze.
■ Lamb not suitable to microwave.
  Total fat: 55.4 grams.
■ Fat per serve: 9.3 grams.

♥ ♥ ♥

MIXED GREEN SALAD

Make recipe just before serving.

2 zucchini, chopped
½lb fresh asparagus, chopped
6 cups (½ bunch) chicory leaves
3 cups (¼ bunch) watercress sprigs
1 radicchio lettuce

DRESSING
1 cup no oil French dressing
4 teaspoons olive oil
3 tablespoons chopped fresh tarragon
½ teaspoon cracked black peppercorns
½ teaspoon sugar
2 teaspoons seeded mustard
4 teaspoons no-added-salt tomato paste

Boil, steam or microwave zucchini and asparagus until just tender, rinse under cold water; drain. Combine all vegetables in bowl, add dressing; toss lightly.
Dressing: Combine all ingredients in bowl; whisk until combined.

Serves 6.

  Total fat: 18 grams.
■ Fat per serve: 3 grams.

♥ ♥ ♥

SORBET PASTRY RINGS WITH BUTTERSCOTCH SAUCE

Recipe can be made 3 days ahead.

2 teaspoons polyunsaturated margarine
1 cup water
⅔ cup self-rising flour
4 egg whites, lightly beaten

ORANGE SORBET
2 cups water
3 tablespoons sugar
⅓ cup fresh lemon juice
1⅓ cups concentrated orange juice
2 egg whites

BUTTERSCOTCH SAUCE
1 cup dark brown sugar, lightly packed
⅓ cup skim milk
2 teaspoons polyunsaturated margarine

Combine margarine and water in pan, bring to boil. Add sifted flour all at once. Stir vigorously over heat until smooth. Place in small bowl of electric mixer. Add egg whites gradually, beat on low speed after each addition. Mixture will separate, but will come together with further beating.

Spoon mixture into piping bag fitted with ½ inch plain tube. Pipe 6 x 4 inch circles of mixture onto baking paper-covered baking sheet. Bake in 400°F oven 10 minutes, reduce heat to 350°F, bake further 15 minutes or until well browned; cool. When pastry rings are cold, cut in half, scoop out any uncooked mixture; discard.

Fill pastry rings with sorbet, freeze until firm. Serve with warm sauce and extra fruit, if desired.
Orange Sorbet: Combine water, sugar and lemon juice in pan, stir over heat until sugar is dissolved. Bring to boil, simmer, uncovered, without stirring, 2 minutes. Stir in orange juice; pour into freezer tray, cover, freeze until just beginning to set. Stir sorbet with fork in bowl until mushy. Beat egg whites in small bowl until soft peaks form, fold into sorbet mixture.
Butterscotch Sauce: Combine sugar, milk and margarine in pan, bring to boil, boil 1 minute.

Serves 6.

■ Suitable to freeze.
■ Not suitable to microwave.
  Total fat: 16.7 grams.
■ Fat per serve: 2.8 grams.

BELOW: Jellied Beets with Chive Dressing.

Glossary

Some terms, names and alternatives are included here
to help everyone understand and use our recipes perfectly.

ALCOHOL: is optional but gives a particular flavor. You can use fruit juice or water instead to make up the liquid content in our recipes.

ALLSPICE: pimento in ground form.

ARROWROOT: is made from a combination of starchy extracts from the roots of various tropical plants, it is used mostly for thickening. Cornstarch can be substituted.

BAKING PAPER: has a nonstick coating which eliminates the need to grease the paper.

DOUBLE-ACTING BAKING POWDER: raising agent made from an alkali and acid. It is mostly made from cream of tartar and baking soda in the proportion of 1 level teaspoon cream of tartar to ½ level teaspoon baking soda. This is equal to 2 level teaspoons double-acting baking powder.

BAKING WARE, NONSTICK: the surface of baking sheets, baking pans, muffin tins, etc, is treated so baked goods turn out easily without greasing.

BARLEY, ROLLED: grains are rolled flat, similar to old-fashioned oats.

BEANS
Black: fermented, salted soy beans. Use either canned or dried. Drain and rinse the canned variety, soak and rinse the dried variety. Leftover beans will keep for months in the refrigerator. Mash beans when cooking to release flavor.
Black-eyed: also known as black-eyed peas.
Green: French beans.
Mexicana chili: canned pinto beans with chili flavoring, several brands are available.

BOK CHOY (CHINESE CHARD): discard stems, use leaves and young tender parts of stems; requires a short cooking time.

BOUILLON CUBE: 1 small bouillon cube is equivalent to 1 teaspoon powdered bouillon; 1 large bouillon cube is equivalent to 2 teaspoons bouillon powder. These are approximate guides.

BRAN, UNPROCESSED: the outer husk of wheat.

BREAD
Pita pocket: unleavened bread which puffs up during cooking, leaving a hollow in the center.
Whole-wheat: we used whole-wheat sliced bread.

BREAD CRUMBS
Packaged unseasoned: commercially packaged unseasoned bread crumbs.

Fresh: we used 1- or 2-day-old white or whole-wheat bread made into crumbs by grating, blending or processing.

BULGUR (CRACKED WHEAT): has been cracked by boiling then re-dried.

CHEESE
Lowfat cottage: soft, fresh white cheese made from skim milk.
Parmesan: very hard cheese available grated or by the piece.
Reduced fat mozzarella: we used a mozzarella with about 14% fat content.
Reduced fat ricotta: a lowfat, fresh, unripened cheese made from whey obtained in the manufacture of other cheese.
Reduced fat cheddar: we used a reduced fat natural cheddar cheese with a fat content of about 17%.

CHILIES, FRESH: are available in many types and sizes. The small ones (birds's eye or bird peppers) are the hottest. Use tight-fitting gloves when handling and chopping the fresh chilies as they can burn your skin. The seeds are the hottest part so remove them if you want to reduce the heat content of a recipe.

CHILI POWDER: the Asian variety is the hottest and is made from ground red chilies; it can be used as a substitute for fresh chilies in the proportion of ½ teaspoon ground chili powder to 1 medium chili.

COLESLAW DRESSING: we used a reduced fat product.

CORNMEAL: ground corn; is similar to yellow cornmeal but is finer and paler. One cannot be substituted for the other as cooking times vary.

CORNMEAL, YELLOW: made from ground corn; is coarser and darker than cornmeal.

COUSCOUS: a fine cereal made from semolina.

CREAM
Light sour: a reduced fat, commercially cultured sour cream.

CUSTARD POWDER: pudding mix.

DAMPER: is an Australian yeast-free quick bread.

EGG ROLL SKINS: are sold frozen; thaw before using, keep covered with a damp cloth while using.

EXTRACT
Coffee and chicory: a slightly bitter syrup based on sugar, caramel, coffee and chicory.
Vanilla: we used an imitation extract.

FLOUR
Buckwheat: flour milled from buckwheat.
White self-rising: substitute all-purpose flour and double-acting baking powder, sift together several times before using. Use 1 cup white all-purpose flour to 2 level teaspoons double-acting baking powder.
Whole-wheat self-rising: if unavailable, add double-acting baking powder to whole-wheat flour as above to make whole-wheat self-rising flour.

FRAMBOISE: raspberry-flavored liqueur.

GARAM MASALA: varied combinations of cardamom, cinnamon, cloves, coriander, cumin and nutmeg make this spice which is often used in Indian cooking. Sometimes pepper is used to make a hot variation. Garam masala is available in jars from Asian food stores and speciality stores.

GINGERROOT
Fresh or green: scrape away skin and it is ready to grate, chop or slice.
Glace: gingerroot which has been cooked in a heavy sugar syrup, then dried. Crystallised gingerroot can be substituted for glace gingerroot; rinse off sugar with water, dry before using.

GOLDEN RAISINS: dried seedless grapes.

GOW GEES PASTRY: are sold frozen; thaw before using, keep, covered, with a damp cloth while using. Available from Asian food stores.

GRAND MARNIER: an orange-flavored liqueur.

GREASING: we used a commercial nonstick spray to grease baking pans.

GREEN ONIONS: also known as scallions.

HERBS: we have specified when to use fresh, ground or dried herbs. We used dried (not ground) herbs in the proportion of 1:4 for fresh herbs, e.g. 1 teaspoon dried herbs instead of 4 teaspoons chopped fresh herbs.

LENTILS: there are many types; all require soaking before cooking, except for red lentils which are ready for cooking without soaking.

MAYONNAISE: we used a reduced fat mayonnaise.

MELON, HONEYDEW: an oval melon with delicate taste and pale green flesh.

MILK
Buttermilk: a cultured product, made by adding culture to skim milk to give a slightly acid flavor. Use skim milk if buttermilk is unavailable.
Nonfat dry milk: dried milk powder which has minimal butterfat.

Skim milk: milk from which the butterfat has been almost completely removed.

NOODLES, EGG: are usually sold in compressed bundles and have been pre-cooked by steaming so they need only minimal preparation at home.

OATS, OLD-FASHIONED: have the husks ground off and are then steam-softened and rolled flat.

OIL
Olive: ripe olives are pressed to obtain olive oil. The best oil comes from the first pressing.
Polyunsaturated: edible vegetable oil.

PAVLOVA: an Australian dessert made from meringue.

PIMIENTOS: sweet red peppers preserved in brine in cans or jars.

POLYUNSATURATED MARGARINE: made from polyunsaturated fats found in vegetable oils. Flavorings, colors and vitamins A and D are usually added.

PUMPKIN SQUASH: any type of pumpkin squash can be substituted for butternut squash or golden nugget squash.

RICE: can be brown or white.
Basmati: a delicately flavored rice from Pakistan, white long-grain rice can be substituted.
Red: a long-grain type of rice with red husks available from Asian food stores.
Rice cake: a gluten and wheat-free product. Rice cakes are a light and crunchy wholegrain crisp flat cake made from rice, corn and water.
Wild: from North America; it is not a member of the rice family. It is expensive as it is difficult to cultivate and has a distinctive flavor.

SAUCE
Chili: we used a hot Chinese variety consisting of chilies, salt and vinegar. We used it sparingly so you can easily increase the amounts in recipes to suit your taste.
Cranberry: cranberries preserved in sugar syrup; has an astringent flavor.
Fish: this sauce is an essential ingredient in the cooking of a number of South-East Asian countries, including Thailand and Vietnam. It is made from the liquid drained from salted, fermented anchovies. It has a strong smell and taste. Use sparingly until you acquire the taste.
Oyster-flavored: a rich, brown bottled sauce made from oysters cooked in salt and soy sauce.
Soy: made from fermented soy beans. The light variety is generally used with white meat dishes. The dark is generally used for color, and the light for flavor.
Sweet chili: a piquant mix of sugar, chili, vinegar, salt and spices. Use sparingly.
Tabasco: made with vinegar, hot red peppers and salt. Use sparingly.

SAMBAL OELEK: also spelt ulek and olek, is a paste made from chilies and salt; use as an ingredient or accompaniment.

SEA SCALLOPS: we used sea scallops with the orange roe attached.

SEGMENTING: cutting citrus fruits in such a way that the pieces contain no pith, seed or membrane. The thickly peeled fruit is cut towards the center inside each membrane, forming wedges.

SEMOLINA: a cereal made from the coarsely ground endosperms of hard durum wheat. Used in puddings, cakes, desserts and some savory dishes.

SNOW PEAS: also known as Chinese pea pods.

SPICE: Chinese assorted, packaged mixed spices available from Asian food stores.

SPINACH: a soft-leaved vegetable, delicate in taste. Young, tender Swiss chard leaves can be substituted for spinach.

STUFFING MIX (seasoned): a tasty packaged mix containing bread crumbs and flavorings.

SUGAR
Granulated: fine granulated table sugar.
Confectioners' sugar: powdered sugar.

SWEET POTATO: we used an orange colored sweet potato.

SWISS CHARD: a large-leafed vegetable; remove coarse white stems, cook green leafy parts.

SYRUP
Corn: available in supermarkets, delicatessens and natural food stores. It is available in light or dark; either can be substituted for the other.
Grenadine: nonalcoholic flavoring made from pomegranate juice; bright red in color. Imitation cordial is also available.
Maple: we used Grade A Dark Amber Maple Syrup.

TAHINI (SESAME PASTE): made from crushed sesame seeds; it is widely used as a flavoring in Middle Eastern and Latin American cookery.

TANGERINES: a variety of mandarin with deeper, orange-red skin which is easily peeled; generally very sweet and juicy.

TEMPEH: is produced by a natural culture of soy beans; has a chunky chewy texture.

TOASTING: almonds and shredded coconut can be toasted in the oven. Spread them evenly onto a baking sheet, toast in 350°F oven about 5 minutes. Desiccated coconut and sesame seeds toast more evenly by stirring over heat in a heavy dry skillet. The natural oils will brown these ingredients.

TOFU: is made from boiled, crushed soy beans to give a type of milk. A coagulant is added, much like the process of cheese making. We used soft tofu and firm tofu. Tofu is easily digested, nutritious and has a slightly nutty flavor. Buy it as fresh as possible; keep any leftover tofu in the refrigerator under water, which must be changed daily.

TOMATO
Paste: a concentrated tomato puree used in soups, stews, sauces, etc. We used a no-added-salt variety.
Puree: canned pureed tomatoes.
Ketchup: we used a no-added-salt variety.
Tomatoes, canned: we used a no-added-salt variety.

VERMOUTH: a wine flavored with a number of different herbs and generally used as an aperitif and in cocktails.

VINEGAR
Cider vinegar: made from fermented apples.
Red wine vinegar: is made from red wine by a slow process, flavored with herbs and spices; it has strong aromatic qualities.
White wine vinegar: made from white wine, flavored with herbs, spices and fruit.

WINE: we used good quality dry red and dry white wines.
Green ginger wine: a sweet white wine infused with crushed fresh gingerroot.

WORCESTSHIRE SAUCE: a dark piquant sauce most commonly used in the UK.

YEAST: allow 2 teaspoons (¼oz) active dry yeast to substitute for ½oz fresh yeast.

YOGURT: we used a lowfat, plain, unflavored yogurt.

CUP & SPOON MEASURES

To ensure accuracy in your recipes use standard measuring equipment.

a) 8 fluid oz cup for measuring liquids.
b) a graduated set of four cups – measuring 1 cup, half, third and quarter cup – for items such as flour, sugar, etc.
When measuring in these fractional cups level off at the brim.
c) a graduated set of five spoons: tablespoon (½ fluid oz liquid capacity), teaspoon, half, quarter and eighth teaspoons.
All spoon measurements are level.

We have used large eggs with an average weight of 2oz each in all our recipes.

Index